The American Crisis Series

Books on the Civil War Era

Steven E. Woodworth, Assistant Professor of History,
Texas Christian University
SERIES EDITOR

～ The Civil War was the crisis of the Republic's first century —the test, in Abraham Lincoln's words, of whether any free government could long endure. It touched with fire the hearts of a generation, and its story has fired the imaginations of every generation since. This series offers to students of the Civil War, either those continuing or those just beginning their exciting journey into the past, concise overviews of important persons, events, and themes in that remarkable period of America's history.

Volumes Published

James L. Abrahamson. *The Men of Secession and Civil War, 1859–1861* (2000). Cloth ISBN 0-8420-2818-8   Paper ISBN 0-8420-2819-6

Robert G. Tanner. *Retreat to Victory? Confederate Strategy Reconsidered* (2001). Cloth ISBN 0-8420-2881-1   Paper ISBN 0-8420-2882-X

Stephen Davis. *Atlanta Will Fall: Sherman, Joe Johnston, and the Yankee Heavy Battalions* (2001). Cloth ISBN 0-8420-2787-4 Paper ISBN 0-8420-2788-2

Paul Ashdown and Edward Caudill. *The Mosby Myth: A Confederate Hero in Life and Legend* (2002). Cloth ISBN 0-8420-2928-1 Paper ISBN 0-8420-2929-X

Spencer C. Tucker. *A Short History of the Civil War at Sea* (2002). Cloth ISBN 0-8420-2867-6   Paper ISBN 0-8420-2868-4

Richard Bruce Winders. *Crisis in the Southwest: The United States, Mexico, and the Struggle over Texas* (2002). Cloth ISBN 0-8420-2800-5   Paper ISBN 0-8420-2801-3

Ethan S. Rafuse. *A Sin͏ ͏ ͏ ͏ The First Campaign and Battle of Manassas (20͏ ͏ Paper ISBN 0-8420-

D1114049

A Short History of
the Civil War at Sea

A Short History of the Civil War at Sea

The American Crisis Series
BOOKS ON THE CIVIL WAR ERA
NO. 5

Spencer C. Tucker

A Scholarly Resources Inc. Imprint
Wilmington, Delaware

Scholarly Resources Inc.
104 Greenhill Avenue
Wilmington, DE 19805-1897
www.scholarly.com

Maps prepared by Dr. Donald Frazier.

Library of Congress Cataloging-in-Publication Data

Tucker, Spencer, 1937–
    A short history of the Civil War at sea / Spencer C. Tucker.
        p. cm. — (The American crisis series ; no. 5)
    Includes bibliographical references and index.
    ISBN 0-8420-2867-6 (alk. paper) — ISBN 0-8420-2868-4 (pbk. :
alk. paper)
    1. United States—History—Civil War, 1861–1865—Naval
operations. I. Title. II. Series.

E591 .T83 2001
973.7'5—dc21   2001032268

For my granddaughter

Cathryn Carter McElroy

About the Author

Spencer C. Tucker holds the John Biggs Chair of Military History at the Virginia Military Institute, Lexington. He is the author or editor of sixteen books on naval and military history and has written two other works on the Civil War at sea: *Raphael Semmes and the Alabama* (1996) and *Andrew Foote: Civil War Admiral on Western Waters* (2000).

CONTENTS

INTRODUCTION

NEARLY 150 YEARS after its conclusion the Civil War continues to attract historians and the general public. Most of this fascination has been directed toward the fighting on land, and there is much to capture the attention, including the exploits of some of America's greatest generals, such as Robert E. Lee, Stonewall Jackson, Ulysses S. Grant, and William T. Sherman. But there were strong and effective leaders at sea, including David G. Farragut, Andrew H. Foote, Franklin Buchanan, and Raphael Semmes. Whereas the struggle at sea—the blue-water Civil War—was nowhere nearly as sanguinary as the contest on land, it is every bit as intriguing.

Students of the Civil War continue to be fascinated by its machinery, especially that used at sea. Of particular appeal are the new Dahlgren guns; the ironclads *Monitor* and *Virginia* and their clash at Hampton Roads, the first ever between ironclads; the extensive use of mines, or torpedoes as they were known at the time and identified here; and the development of submarines, one of which registered history's first successful sinking of a surface ship by a submerged vessel.

There also were dramatic major sea battles, although the numbers of ships involved did not approach those at Trafalgar in 1805, or in the later battles of Jutland in 1916, or Leyte Gulf in 1944. An advantage for the student of the war, the smaller numbers make it possible to examine the battles in greater detail. Single ship contests also attract attention—primarily the *Monitor* versus the *Virginia*—but also the *Kearsarge* versus the *Alabama*. Sea battles were not most of the war, of course. Typical of other conflicts, the bulk of a sailor's time was occupied with routine activities. There were long stretches of monotony, punctuated by a few episodes of intense and dramatic action.

The war at sea was immensely important in deciding the outcome. The North was able to exploit its significant naval and maritime advantage to turn the war on land in its favor. Above all there was the Union blockade of the Confederate coasts. This action kept the South from selling its cotton crop abroad and using the revenue to purchase arms and machinery. Although blockade runners continued to get into Southern ports throughout the war, it became much more difficult as the conflict wore on, and much of this traffic, in any case, was not in war matériel. Control of the Confederate coasts afforded the Union the same advantage that the British had enjoyed during the War of American Independence and again in the War of 1812—the ability to project land forces at will against any point along some thirty-five hundred miles of coastline. Such actions intensified the South's already horrendous defensive problems, forcing it to dissipate scant resources over a vast area.

Union control of the sea also prevented foreign intervention in the war, a major goal of President Abraham Lincoln's diplomacy. There was another side to the blockade, too little mentioned. Union sea power allowed the North access to the world's markets. It not only permitted the United States to secure what it needed for the war from abroad, but it also allowed the North to sell its products to Europe and the rest of the world. Such activities strengthened the Northern economy. "Corn," as the English called grain, shipped from the North was more important to Britain than cotton. Of course, Confederate commerce raiders usually destroyed a number of Union merchant ships, thereby driving up insurance rates and forcing the fleet of ships to fly foreign flags. However, it did not affect Union trade to any appreciable extent.

In the interior, Union land and naval forces, working in tandem, bisected the South along its great interior rivers. Southern ironclads along these rivers were few in number and too indifferently propelled to be a major factor. Northern control over the Mississippi River, when it came at last, had profound political and economic influences, as well as the obvious military advantage of cutting off supplies from the Trans-Mississippi West to the remainder of the Confederacy.

Union naval forces, sometimes operating alone and at other times working with U.S. Army troops, seized many Southern coastal strongholds, including Port Royal, New Orleans, Hatteras Inlet, and Roanoke Island. Some ports, such as Charleston and Wilmington, held out much longer. Charleston was the scene of one of the more dramatic confrontations of the war and one of the most sustained operations in naval history. The Union seizure of Confederate ports cut them off as a point for blockaders but reduced the land and sea power of the Confederacy and furnished bases for future Union operations. Sometimes Union naval forces operated independently, such as Commodore Farragut's operations against Vicksburg.

Further, ships engaged shore and river batteries on numerous occasions. In some cases large vessels operated at close range, such as at Fort Henry on the Tennessee River, in the passage to New Orleans, and against Vicksburg. But there were many more examples of smaller vessels employing boat howitzers at close range to engage a battery or single artillery piece along riverbanks. While ship-to-shore bombardment was not always successful, there were occasions when it was crucial to the outcome, such as at the Battles of Belmont and Shiloh.

Indeed, the Civil War saw extensive use of shore bombardment as a result of many factors, the most important of which was the introduction of ironclad vessels and steam power. The latter allowed bombarding vessels to choose the timing of their attack, independent of wind conditions, and to maintain position much more easily than old sail-driven warships. More accurate and more powerful guns also had appeared, although the effectiveness of these weapons against earthen fortifications was limited.

Although fighting on land continues to hold center stage, much more is being written about the Civil War at sea. The naval war is coming at last to receive the attention it so richly deserves.

CHAPTER ONE

THE SEA WAR BEGINS

MID-NINETEENTH-CENTURY NAVAL REVOLUTION

WHEN THE CIVIL WAR began, a revolution in ships and naval ordnance was under way. The war both benefited from, and enhanced, that change. As far as ships were concerned, the revolution meant a change from wooden vessels propelled by wind to iron ships powered by steam.

Americans had led in the revolution. Robert Fulton's *Demologos* was the world's first steam warship, and John Ericsson and Robert F. Stockton's *Princeton* was the world's first screw propeller warship. Robert L. Stevens, who had begun the ironclad revolution, came up with the idea of attaching iron plates to a vessel to protect it from enemy fire. The Stevens Battery, as it came to be known, was never completed. When Stevens received congressional funding in 1842, it was the first government appropriation in history for a modern ironclad warship, but then Ericsson arrived in the United States with a 12-inch gun. Tests with this powerful gun confirmed that its projectiles could smash through 4.5 inches of iron. This fact forced Stevens to increase armor thickness to 6.75 inches, and the ship had to be enlarged to take the extra weight. There was talk during the Civil War of completing the Stevens Battery, but the cost was too great, and it was sold for scrap in the 1870s.

Other powers took up the idea, especially the French. Similar to the Confederacy in that their chief rival, the British, possessed overwhelming naval power, the French sought to offset the British advantage by new technology. The effectiveness of ironclads was demonstrated during the 1854–1856 Crimean War. In October 1855 three French floating batteries, armored with 4-inch forged iron over their wooden sides, attacked Russia's Kinburn forts at the mouth of the Dnieper and Bug Rivers and reduced them to rubble. The French vessels were largely undamaged, and many observers concluded that the days of wooden ships-of-the-line were over.

The British also built floating batteries, but it was the French who most fully understood their implications. France halted construction of wooden ships-of-the-line and began converting its fleet into fast, single-gun deck ironclads. In 1858, France laid down the steam screw frigate *Gloire*, which entered service in 1860. Her sails were secondary only. Protected by a 4.5-inch belt of iron that ran her entire length and extended from 6 feet below the waterline to the upper deck, she mounted 30 rifled, breech-loading guns. France launched its first iron-hulled capital ship, the *Couronne*, in March 1861.

The British, however, were slower to act. Although well aware of the new developments, London continued to build wooden ships-of-the-line. The British did not have great confidence in ironclad vessels. Indeed, in 1856 they responded to the U.S. Navy's new large *Merrimack* class of steam frigates with the *Mersey* and *Orlando*, the largest and most powerful single-deck wooden warships ever built. But news of the construction of the *Gloire*, which reached Britain in May 1858, created something akin to panic and goaded London into action. Britain led the world in metallurgical techniques, and its armor plate was superior to that of France.

The result of Britain's advanced shipbuilding techniques was the *Warrior* of 1862. She demonstrated British determination to retain leadership in naval technology. She was larger than the *Gloire* and longer than any wooden warship. Whereas her rival was merely a wooden ship protected by iron plate, the *Warrior* was virtually an iron vessel. Whereas the *Gloire* was designed for coastal purposes, the English ship was an ocean-going warship. The *Warrior* immediately made every other warship in the world obsolete. By 1861, Britain and France had a total of twenty-eight ironclads built or under construction.

Armored turrets to encase the guns on ships also appeared. As early as 1843, T. R. Timby of New York had patented the metallic revolving fort for use on either land or ship. Capt. Cowper Coles of the Royal Navy developed the same idea during the Crimean War and perfected it by 1858. His turret, based on a railroad turntable, was mounted on a roller path (John Ericsson's turret design for the *Monitor* utilized a central pivot instead). Combined with iron hulls, the turret allowed small vessels to mount a few of the heaviest guns.

A revolution also was under way in types of projectiles and ordnance. For centuries the mainstay at sea had been solid shot projected from smoothbore muzzle-loading guns. Shot tended to leave smooth round holes that were easy to patch, and few ships were actually sunk by it. Rather, it was personnel casualties and the damaging of masts and spars by shot that tended to be fatal. Probably more ships were taken by boarding than were sunk. In the 1820s, however, individuals, especially Col. Henri Paixhans in France, had become advocates of explosive shell. Paixhans and others argued that guns should be developed to project large shells at sufficient velocity so that they would lodge in the side of the target wooden vessel and then explode, tearing large irregular holes that would be difficult to patch and that perhaps would even sink the intended victim.

Commander John Dahlgren was the principal ordnance innovator in the U.S. Navy before the Civil War, and in 1844 he had been assigned to the Washington Navy Yard to conduct ordnance ranging experiments. Soon he was designing locks for guns and had developed a new system of naval ordnance. In 1849 he produced a new howitzer for the navy. Cast of bronze, these appeared as 12- and 24-pounder smoothbores and 3.4-inch (12-pounder) and 4-inch (20-pounder) rifles. The boat howitzers were the finest guns of their time in the world. Extensively used by both sides throughout the Civil War, they remained in service with the U.S. Navy until the 1880s. They also were copied by other navies. But Dahlgren is chiefly remembered for his system of heavy smoothbore, muzzle-loading ordnance. The first prototype 9-inch Dahlgren gun was cast at Pittsburgh's Fort Pitt Foundry and delivered to the Washington Navy Yard in May 1850.

The new guns, with their smooth exterior, curved lines, and weight of metal at the breech, which was the point of greatest strain, resembled soda water bottles and were sometimes so called. Dahlgren designed them to place the greatest weight of metal at the point of greatest strain at the breech. The 9-inch remained the most common broadside, carriage-mounted gun in the U.S. Navy in the Civil War; the 11-inch, the prototype of which was cast in 1851, was the most widely used pivot-mounted gun. A shell from the latter could pierce 4.5 inches of plate iron backed by 20 inches of solid oak.

Dahlgren guns appeared in a variety of sizes including 32-pounder, 8-inch, 9-inch, 10-inch (a lighter gun for shell and heavier gun for firing primarily shot), 11-inch, 13-inch, and 15-inch. The latter weighed 42,000 pounds. There was even a gun of 22-inch bore (97,300 pounds) that did not see service aboard ship during the war, however. The 15-inchers were used aboard Union monitors. Dahlgren also designed rifled guns, somewhat similar in shape to his smoothbores. Some of these had separate bronze trunnion and breech straps. Dahlgren rifles appeared in 4.4-inch (30-pounder), 5.1-inch (50-pounder), 6-inch (80-pounder), 7.5-inch (150-pounder), and 12-inch (only three of which were cast). They were not successful, and in February 1862 most were withdrawn from service. Apart from the rifles, Dahlgren guns were extraordinarily reliable. Ironically, in the Civil War the best chance of damaging an ironclad was with a smoothbore gun firing solid shot, not shell, at the greatest possible velocity.

Old guns and truck carriages were widely used during the war, as may be seen in the photograph of U.S. Navy steam tug *Thomas Freeborn* of the Potomac Flotilla in May 1861. Naval Historical Center. NH 60990

The most reliable rifled guns on the Union side were those designed by Robert P. Parrott, former army ordnance captain and then superintendent of the West Point Foundry Association, one of the major suppliers of ordnance to the army and navy. Rifled guns were extremely vulnerable to bursting because of closer tolerance and greater strain on the gun in burning the powder charge. Recognizing the vulnerability of the cast-iron tube, Parrott shrunk a hot wrought-iron spiral-wound band over the breech of the gun. On cooling, it contracted and gripped the tube with its tensile strength.

Parrott's first rifle was a 2.9-inch (10-pounder), but before the Civil War he also made a 3.67-inch (20-pounder) and a 4.2-inch (30-pounder). After the start of the war larger Parrotts were manufactured for both the U.S. Army and Navy. These appeared in 5.3-inch (60-pounder), 6.4-inch (100-pounder), 8-inch (150-pounder), and 10-inch (300-pounder) sizes. By February 1864 the navy had received 790 Parrott guns, from 3.67- to 8-inch size,

A 6.4-inch (100-pounder) Parrott rifled gun aboard USS *Teaser* during the Civil War. Note the compressor gear and shell in the foreground. National Archives. 90-CR1-482

representing about one-fifth the inventory of U.S. Navy guns. Parrotts were easy to operate, durable, and inexpensive enough that they could be produced in large quantities.

The Confederates cast their own versions of these guns and had in Lt. John Mercer Brooke a superlative ordnance designer. He produced 32-pounder, 10- and 11-inch smoothbores, probably based on standard U.S. Navy patterns, but also 6.4-inch, 7-inch, and 8-inch rifled guns, the last named probably the best of the war on either side. Somewhat thicker than the Parrotts in appearance, they differed from them in having a second and even a third series of wrought-iron bands, made up of a succession of rings, over the cast-iron tube.

SHIPS AND THE BALANCE OF FORCES

The North had virtually all the advantages. One clear edge was in population. Whereas in 1776 the North and South had been approximately equal, by the time of the Civil War the North had twenty-two million people; the South had but nine million, and over one-third of these were slaves.

If the Civil War was the first industrial war, the South was woefully unprepared for it, thus affecting the naval sphere more than on land. In 1861 the North had some 85 percent of total U.S. manufacturing. The entire South had less manufacturing capacity than New York City; it had no facilities for forging steel, nor could it construct machine tools. Four of the five large prewar foundries capable of casting the heaviest iron guns were in the North. The single such facility in the South, the Tredegar Iron Works in Richmond, Virginia, did not use the Rodman Process, acclaimed as the most advanced technique for producing the strongest guns.

The world's navies had entered a new industrial age, and the South had serious problems building the steam engines to power the new ironclad vessels. Only the Tredegar could manufacture entire propulsion systems. Most of the steam engines that powered Confederate naval vessels were requisitioned from civilian vessels, and throughout the war the vast majority of new Confederate naval construction was inadequately powered. Given the vast difference in manufacturing capacity between North and South, it is hardly surprising that the war turned out as it did.

The South had iron and coal deposits, and an abundance of timber, but transportation facilities to bring raw materials to manufacturing sites were wholly inadequate. Only Richmond, New Orleans, and Memphis had properly equipped civilian facilities that could, given the opportunity, construct and repair ironclad vessels. Eight of ten prewar navy yards were in the North, and the largest yard, at Gosport (Norfolk), was retaken from the South in 1862. The two navy yards of Pensacola and Norfolk, which fell into Confederate hands, never produced up to their capacity while under Southern control.

Although the South was inferior to the North by virtually all military measures, it had one great advantage. To win the war, the North would have to conquer the South. To uphold its independence, the South would simply have to avoid losing.

At the outset, both sides were in fact militarily weak. The U.S. Army was small and scattered. When the war began in April 1861 the Northerners did enjoy a clear advantage at sea. The U.S. Navy had but ninety ships and most were in ordinary (reserve, equivalent to today's mothballing) or acting as receiving ships; only forty-two were in commission. Thirty of those in commission were widely scattered: in Asia, South America, and off the African coast suppressing the slave trade. Only four were in Northern waters. Even concentrated, the number of ships was totally inadequate for what lay ahead.

Largely because of Northern manufacturing superiority, the U.S. Navy grew rapidly. Within eight months it had 135 ships and had contracted for the construction of 52 others. By December 1864 the navy had grown to nearly 671 vessels of all types, totaling 510,396 tons and armed with 4,610 guns. Its fleet included 113 screw steamers especially constructed for naval purposes; 52 paddle-wheel steamers especially constructed for naval purposes; 71 ironclads; 323 steamers, either purchased or captured, fitted for naval purposes; and 112 sailing vessels of all kinds. Of the 671 vessels, the overwhelming majority (559) were powered by steam. These numbers made the U.S. Navy the largest in the world, next to that of Great Britain.

One interesting aspect of the war was the large number of African Americans in the U.S. Navy. Eager to secure and maintain that important source of manpower, the navy granted unparalleled social equality to its black sailors, although it did restrict their tasks aboard ship. It also offered the same pay for blacks and whites, and they shared equally in prize money distributions. One estimate is that twenty-four thousand African Americans were in the Union navy, about 16 percent of its total strength. Blacks also may have been attracted by better conditions. For example, the U.S. Army lost roughly one in every fifteen recruits to disease, while the navy lost only one in forty. Death rates in combat were one in nine for the army but only one in sixty-five for the navy.

The war also saw the first hospital ships in U.S. Navy history. In March 1862 the *Ben Morgan* was converted from a hulk into a hospital ship with the North Atlantic Squadron. In December 1862 the navy also placed in commission the former Confederate steamer *Red Rover* in the Mississippi Squadron. She featured two operating rooms, a special space for amputations, an elevator to shift patients between desks, and several flush toilets. She also achieved another first for a U.S. Navy ship by taking aboard female nurses from the Order of the Holy Cross.

On its formation the Confederacy did not even have a navy, let alone a secretary of the navy. The South had not a single warship of importance, and it had only one prewar navy yard—Pensacola in Florida. Of modest size and more a coaling and repair station than anything else, Pensacola was effectively neutralized by the Federal occupation, by reinforcement of Fort Pickens on Santa Rosa Island, and by a Union blockading squadron. The Union controlled Fort Pickens throughout the war, and in any case, a Union blockading squadron closed off Pensacola Bay.

With secession, Southern militias seized the Federal arsenals on their territory as well as many of the key coastal forts, including Moultrie in Charleston Harbor, Fort Pulaski off Georgia, Forts Gaines and Morgan in Mobile Bay, Caswell near Wilmington, North Carolina, and both St. Philip and Jackson below New Orleans. The most important of these assets came on the secession of Virginia. On April 20, 1861, the Confederacy gained control of the largest prewar U.S. Navy yard at Gosport (Norfolk). Although withdrawing Union troops tried to destroy the facility and its stores, the South secured some twelve hundred heavy guns, including fifty-two 9-inch Dahlgrens, and significant quantities of naval stores and some vessels. Among the latter was the powerful modern steam frigate *Merrimack*. Although retreating Union forces had set her afire, she burned only to the waterline before sinking. The Confederates promptly raised her and began rebuilding her as an ironclad. The North, however, retained Fortress Monroe at the entrance of Hampton Roads and held it throughout the war. It proved a useful enclave and staging area.

Confederate President Jefferson Davis paid only little attention to naval matters. This former highly effective secretary of war did not understand the role a navy might play in securing a Southern victory. Certainly he was in no rush to build and secure ships. Fortunately, he did have a highly effective secretary of the navy, Stephen R. Mallory. A former U.S. senator from Florida, he had chaired the Naval Committee.

The Confederate navy hardly enjoyed an auspicious beginning. Mallory inherited just five vessels from the seceded states. He also secured through seizure or purchase four revenue cutters, three slavers, two privately owned coastal steamers, and the side-wheeler *Fulton*, laid up at the Pensacola Navy Yard. As with the U.S. Navy, the Confederates also purchased merchant steamers for conversion into warships.

The South did benefit from many capable former U.S. Navy officers. In the spring of 1861 there were 571 officers in the U.S. Navy (captains, commanders, and lieutenants). Of these, 253 (44.3 percent) were born in the South and one-half (126) resigned to go with the Confederacy. The remainder, a majority of one, stayed with the U.S. flag. In all respects, Confederate naval practices closely followed those of the Union. The Confederate ordnance manual, for example, was a virtual copy of that for the U.S. Navy.

Although no cruisers were built in Confederate ports during the war, the Confederacy did construct a great many wooden gunboats. These vessels fell into three broad categories: a class of at least four large side-wheel steamers, three classes of screw steamers designed by Confederate Chief Naval Constructor John L. Porter, and a variety of small vessels conceived by oceanographer and former U.S. Navy officer Matthew Fontaine Maury and intended for coast defense.

The first category of ships included the *Bienville, Carondelet, Gaines,* and *Morgan.* The first two, constructed at New Orleans, were built to help protect that city against Federal attack but fell prey to Flag Officer David Farragut's Gulf Coast Squadron. The *Bienville* was destroyed in Lake Pontchartrain on April 21, 1862, prior to completion, to prevent capture. The *Carondelet* fought in the Battle of Pass Christian on April 4, 1862, and also was destroyed on the 21st to prevent capture. The other two side-wheel steamers were constructed at Mobile in 1862 as part of the Confederate squadron guarding Mobile Bay. Both fought in the August 5, 1864, Battle of Mobile Bay. The *Gaines* was run aground, while the *Morgan* escaped upriver and was not taken until the fall of the city of Mobile on May 4, 1865.

Ten Porter-designed gunboats were built. Some 110' to 150' in length x 10' depth of hold, they were both sail and steam powered. As with all Confederate warships, steam power plants varied widely, even with specific classes, and many if not most were underpowered. The *Macon,* one of the largest of the Porter designs, was 150' (overall length) x 25' x 8'. Armed with 1 x 9-inch Dahlgren, 4 x 32-pounder smoothbores, and 1 x 32-pounder rifled gun, she participated in the defense of Savannah and was surrendered at Augusta, Georgia, in May 1865. The Porter gunboats, though small, rendered effective service but were employed mostly as auxiliaries.

Maury's gunboats were by far the most extensive Confederate shipbuilding program of the war. Despite Mallory's well-known interest in building ironclads, Maury's political influence in December 1861 secured Confederate congressional approval for construction of 100 gunboats. It was reminiscent of Thomas Jefferson's program at the beginning of the century for 170 small gunboats that had proven largely ineffective in the War of 1812. Maury believed that the South lacked the ability to build larger ships, and he assumed that his small, easily built, relatively inexpensive, light-draft steam gunboats, when armed with two to four guns each, would be a match for larger Union warships.

The Maury gunboats were not to have cabins or accommodations on board. They were 106' to 116' x 18' to 21' x 6.5'. Fifteen *Hampton*-class Maury gunboats were laid down but only five were completed; the rest were burned on the stocks. They mounted two guns: a rifled 32-pounder forward and a 9-inch Dahlgren smoothbore aft. Other Maury gunboats were started at Pensacola, Edwards Ferry, and Elizabeth City, North Carolina, but these were destroyed before they could be manned or completed. These gunboats turned out to be too small to combat the larger Union warships, and those that were completed ended up as auxiliaries.

UNION BLOCKADE

Although the Civil War witnessed no great fleet engagements, the naval war was vital to the outcome and is a prime example of the importance of command of the sea. The North controlled the sea at all points during the war, and this dominance continued to grow during the conflict. At the onset, each side had different goals at sea. The chief Union goal was to impose a blockade and police some thirty-five hundred miles of Confederate coastline. Secondarily, Union leaders hoped to mount amphibious operations along the Confederate coasts and on the interior great western rivers where roads were few and inadequate. Then, as the war continued, the Union was forced to send out increasing numbers of fast cruisers to hunt down and destroy Confederate commerce raiders that were attacking Union merchant ships.

Union Secretary of the Navy Gideon Welles's first and most pressing task, however, was to cut off the South from outside assistance by instituting an effective naval blockade. Ably aided by Assistant Secretary Gustavus Vasa Fox, Welles busied himself converting a relatively small, and for the most part obsolete, collection of ships into an effective force. Welles launched a large naval construction program that included seven ironclads. He relied heavily on Chief of the Bureau of Construction, Equipment, and Repairs John Lenthall and Chief Engineer Benjamin F. Isherwood. But in the short run and for immediate use, government purchasing agents scoured Northern ports, purchasing ships of all types.

As the United States had the world's second largest merchant marine behind only Britain, a great many ships were available, including steamers. The purchased vessels went off to yards, underwent quick conversions, and were assigned to blockade duty. The Union blockade was in fact the first modern blockade, and its power was derived from steam engines. Faster than sailing vessels, steamers could eventually overtake them.

On April 17, 1861, two days after Lincoln called for seventy-five thousand volunteers, Davis issued a proclamation inviting applications for letters of marque and reprisal—that is, privateers. He believed that he was legally free to do this because the United States had not ratified the 1856 Treaty of Paris, under which the signatories forswore the use of privateers. In retaliation, on April 19, Lincoln proclaimed a blockade of the Confederate coasts and warned that any one attacking a U.S. vessel would be treated as a pirate. This threat did not deter applications to Davis for letters of marque, although few of these vessels ever took to the seas.

From Lincoln's point of view the blockade would serve two important functions. First, by sharply reducing the South's access to foreign markets, it would be more difficult for the South to wage war. Second, the blockade demonstrated to foreign powers Lincoln's resolve to crush the rebellion. But the declaration of a blockade could be construed as a de facto recognition of the Confederacy's independent existence, and European states responded by recognition of the South's belligerent rights. Also, according to the Declaration of Paris, foreign powers were not obligated to respect a blockade unless it was effective, that is, maintained by force sufficient to prevent access to an enemy coast.

The Confederacy missed an opportunity at the beginning of the conflict. Although never officially announced as government policy, Davis supported withholding the cotton crop from Europe, and this was done. The assumption was that keeping the cotton at home would force the British to send warships to assist in breaking the Union blockade. However, they did not, and indeed, Queen Victoria issued a proclamation calling on her subjects not to break a legally constituted blockade.

Precious time and a great deal of money were lost as much of the cotton crop rotted on Southern wharves. It should have been rushed to Europe, and the money realized from its sale used to

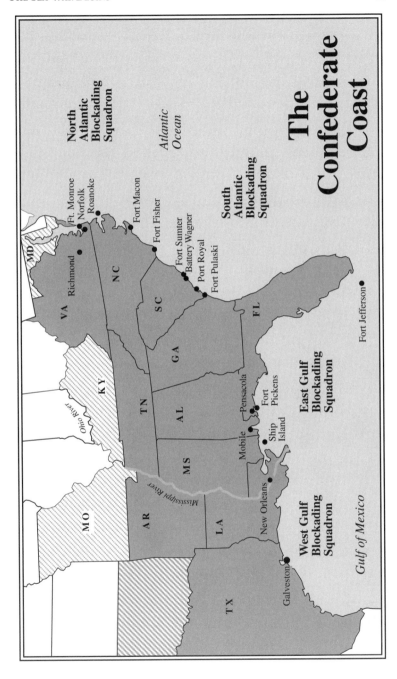

The
Confederate
Coast

purchase and build vessels to break the blockade, as well as arms and steam engines suitable for both ships and locomotives. With gold reserves soon exhausted, the Confederacy reversed its 1861 policy and attempted to ship cotton to pay for goods received.

Although the South did run a fair amount of cotton through the blockade between 1862 and 1865, it was only a small fraction of prewar exports, and increasingly production of cotton was shifted over to food, although not nearly so much as needed. Probably the amount of cotton carried out by blockade runners amounted to no more than 350,000 bales (most of which went out from the southeastern Atlantic coast). Another 50,000 or so went overland through Texas to Mexico, where it was shipped out through Tampico and Matamoras. This trade became so important to the Confederate government that in 1863 it ordered 12 special blockade runners to be built in England for the express purpose of transporting cotton. Each had a capacity of 800 bales, and 6 were still in service at the end of the war.

The blockade runner *A. D. Vance*, whose long, sleek lines were typical of such ships. *ORN*, series 1, vol. 10 (Washington, DC: Government Printing Office, 1900), 453.

The inability of the South to ship out large amounts of its principal product meant that the Confederate government was deprived of its chief source of revenue. Taxes could not be paid and paper money steadily declined in value. This depreciation and the shortage of essential goods meant that prices reached astronomical levels. During 1863 and 1864 the price of a barrel of flour had shot up from $45 to $350 per barrel. Thus, it was difficult to induce blockade runners to bring in essential raw materials or war matériel. Much more money was to be made in items for the consumer economy.

Meanwhile, the North was busy putting together its blockading fleet. Although Welles's steamers-cum-warships were weak as fighting vessels, they were sufficient to deal with the Confederate sail-driven blockade runners. They were essential in blockade operations. Of existing ships the navy had only nineteen steamers in 1860, but most were of new construction. The five heavily gunned first-class screw frigates of the *Merrimack* class and the screw sloop *Niagara* authorized in 1854 were powerful vessels. But size was sometimes a disadvantage in blockade duties. The *Merrimack*-class warships, the *Niagara*, and the large paddle-wheel sloops *Susquehanna* and *Powhatan* drew too much water to be useful for shoal water duty along the Southern coasts.

The U.S. Navy screw sloop *Hartford*. Farragut's flagship during the operation up the Mississippi, she was one of the most famous ships of the war. This photograph was taken during the war. Note sails and laundry drying. Naval Historical Center. NH 90535

Of more use during the Civil War were twelve large sloops of war that Congress authorized in 1857 and 1858. They entered service beginning in 1859 and included the five *Hartford* class, perhaps the best of the Union warships at the start of the war: the *Brooklyn, Hartford, Lancaster, Pensacola,* and *Richmond.* The *Lancaster* served on the Pacific station, but the other four rendered important war service. The *Hartford*, the most famous of these ships, had the longest service life. With their relatively shallow draft and large batteries, these sloops proved invaluable in coastal and riverine operations.

During the war other screw sloops were used for both coastal operations and hunting down Confederate cruisers on the high seas. The two-ship *Mohigan* class, the *Mohigan* and *Kearsarge*, were highly effective vessels. The *Kearsarge* was one of the best-known ships of the war, due to her engagement with the Confederate raider *Alabama*, and she enjoyed a long service life, succumbing only to shipwreck off Central America in 1894. Other screw sloops included the three-vessel *Iroquois* class, two-vessel screw sloop *Wyoming* class, the *Dacotah*, two-vessel *Narragansett* class, and the *Pawnee*. After the start of the war, many additional screw sloops joined the fleet: four *Ossipee* class, two *Canandaigua* class, two *Lackawanna* class, the *Sacramento* and the *Monongahela*, ten *Contookcook* class, eleven *Algoma* class, and six *Swatara* class.

After the Confederates initiated commerce raiding, Welles convened a board of officers to recommend a class of ships to hunt down these vessels. This action resulted in the powerful screw sloop *Sacramento* (1863). In March 1865 she blockaded the Confederate ram *Stonewall* at Ferrol, Spain. In addition to chasing Confederate commerce raiders, the screw sloops were useful in blockade duties and participated in the bombardment of Charleston and Fort Fisher. They also fought in the Battle of Mobile Bay.

With her funnel lowered, only her greater length betrayed the fact that the screw steamer was not a traditional sailing warship. Unlike the paddlers that carried a reduced armament of a few heavier guns on the upper deck and relied on long-range fire, screw steamers could, and did, have traditional broadsides armament; most, however, retained the paddler arrangement of a few heavy guns on the upper deck.

The most pressing need in the blockade, however, was for fast, smaller gunboats capable of operating effectively in coastal shoal water and along rivers. Just one such vessel was available, the *Princeton*. Commissioned in 1852, she was a receiving ship at Philadelphia and continued in that capacity during the war. Isherwood suggested a design used in the construction of two small (691 tons) shallow-draft gunboats built for the Russian Navy to be used along the Amur River.

Within two months the keels of twenty-three of these vessels had been laid down. The first and namesake of this class, the *Unadilla*, was completed in just ninety-three days, leading to the designation of the class as "ninety-day gunboats." All were commissioned by March 1862. The *Unadillas* proved their worth in operations throughout the war, and ten took part in the April 1862 naval engagement preceding the Union capture of New Orleans. They also made 146 captures during the blockade. However, they did have problems. Machinery frequently broke down, steering was sluggish, and their maximum 8- to 9-knot speed was slow for blockade responsibilities.

In August 1862, a second class of eight shallow-draft gunboats was authorized. These *Nipsic*-class (also known as *Kansas*-class) gunboats entered service beginning in December 1863. They performed well during the war, although they did not see extensive service because of their relatively late commissioning date.

By midsummer the Union blockade of the South was well under way. Davis's mistaken belief in the power of cotton caused the South to go slow with its own construction of ships to run the blockade. The potential worth of blockade running was amply demonstrated in September 1861, when a privately owned British vessel, the iron-hulled screw steamer *Bermuda*, arrived from England with eighty-one rifled field pieces, four heavy smoothbore guns, sixty-five hundred Enfield rifles, and twenty thousand cartridges for the Confederate government.

The Confederate government left most of the blockade running to the private sector. As profit in luxury goods was considerably greater than in war supplies, much of the trade was in consumer goods rather than more important military goods. With fortunes to be made on one successful voyage, too often patriotism took second place to the quest for profit. Even the British got involved, organizing private firms for blockade-running operations.

Speedy, low-silhouette ships were built specifically for blockade running. Their powerful engines burning anthracite coal to give off little smoke, blockade runners, painted a slate gray to render them almost invisible, would choose a moonless night to run past Union blockaders. Since Union ships used rockets to signal to consorts the presence of a blockade runner and her direction, sometimes the blockade runners themselves fired decoy signal rockets to draw off the blockaders. Blockade runners sought the protection of shore guns as quickly as possible. As a last resort, a ship could be run aground on the shore, with her cargo salvaged later at some convenient time. When this tactic was used, Union ships would send shore parties to burn her and, if this were not possible, would endeavor to set her afire at a distance with hot shot.

Wilmington and Charleston were the chief ports for blockade running, although Charleston became more difficult for the blockade runners to use with the seizure of Morris Island at the end of 1863 and the fact that Union warships could then watch the narrow harbor entrance from inside the bar. Access to Wilmington on the Cape Fear River was fairly easy because of its separate entrances, at least until Union forces took Fort Fisher in January 1865.

Savannah, another principal blockade-running port, was rendered virtually inaccessible with the Union capture of Fort Pulaski at the harbor entrance by a joint military-naval assault in the summer of 1862. The mouth of the Rio Grande, forming the boundary between Texas and Mexico, was particularly difficult for Union ships to blockade. Cargoes arriving there would be discharged at Matamoras, Mexico, and then transferred by barge to the Texas side. This off-loading could be done without interference by Union seagoing ships because the river was too shallow for them to enter. The goods could then be transported from Texas by rail to any point in the Confederacy, that is, until Union troops secured control of the Mississippi River in 1863.

Most blockade runners got through. One estimate is that 84 percent of those attempting to enter the port of Wilmington were successful, and the ratio was about the same for other Southern ports. Financial rewards could be considerable, even if a ship were to be lost. One blockade runner, lost after eight trips, nonetheless returned a profit of 700 percent. In her eighteen trips through the blockade, the *Herald* took out $3 million (in gold) in cotton, and the *Lee* made twenty-one trips and transported out $2 million in cotton. These amounts do not include profits on goods brought in through the blockade on return trips. Most of the blockade runners were not as fortunate as these, but it does explain why so many individuals sought to participate.

The blockading Union ships were organized into four main squadrons: the North Atlantic Blockading Squadron had responsibility for the Chesapeake Bay, its tributaries, and the coast south to the South Carolina boundary near Wilmington. The South Atlantic Blockading Squadron operated principally from Port Royal, South Carolina. It continued the blockade southward from near Wilmington to Cape Canaveral, Florida. After January 1862 the original Gulf Coast Blockading Squadron was divided into two: the East Gulf Blockading Squadron had responsibility from Cape Canaveral to St. Andrew's Bay, and the West Gulf Blockading Squadron ran from St. Andrew's Bay to the Rio Grande boundary with Mexico.

Blockading duties were tedious and sometimes difficult. Usually the blockade runners attempted to pass in or out in difficult weather conditions, heightening difficulties for the blockading ships. Thus, blockading vessels had to keep on station in all kinds of weather, be it tropical summer heat or in the gales and cold of winter.

As the Union blockade strengthened, the South was forced into reliance on smaller, fast, shallow-draft vessels. Union warships seized ships of any nation (even on the high seas) that could be proved bound for Southern ports. As a result, large ships carried cargoes to Nassau—the favorite destination—to Bermuda, to Havana, or to Halifax. Here their cargoes were transferred to smaller steamers for the run to the South. Union sailors on blockade duty found it difficult, frustrating, and hazardous duty as they were forced to contend with the blockade runners in coastal shoal waters.

About 800 vessels managed to evade the blockade in its first year of operation. By comparison, in 1860, the last year of peace, 6,000 ships had entered and cleared Southern ports. Subsequent Union joint naval and military expeditions helped tighten the blockade. By January 1865 the Union navy had 471 ships with 2,245 guns in blockade service. During the course of the war these ships took a total of about 1,500 vessels of all classes.

Steamers were the most successful blockade runners. From the beginning of the blockade to its end on June 23, 1865, some 300 steamers tested the blockade. Over 1,000 of 1,300 attempts were successful. The average life of one of these blockade runners was just over four runs or two round-trips. During the war 136 were captured and another 85 destroyed.

Although it is true that at no time did Southern armies lack the essential weapons with which to fight and win battles, it is also true that the South was hard-pressed in such essential items as artillery, clothing, shoes, harness, medicines, and even blankets. The loss of rolled iron rail was particularly harmful to the Southern war effort. The gradual deterioration of Confederate railroads led to serious distribution problems, even of food, affecting soldier and civilian alike.

EARLY FIGHTING

The first fighting on land occurred in the east. Union forces secured control of western Virginia, which promptly seceded from Virginia. Hopes in the North of a quick victory were dashed in the First Battle of Manassas (Bull Run) on July 21, 1861, when the Confederates sent attacking Union troops streaming back to Washington. Both sides now settled in for a long war.

In the early months of the war there were numerous small engagements between blockading Union ships and shore batteries. The first of these took place on May 7 when Lt. Thomas O. Selfridge's armed tug the *Yankee*, carrying out a reconnaissance, came under fire from a Confederate shore battery off Gloucester Point in the York River. During May 29 and June 1 the three Union steamers *Thomas Freeborn*, *Anacostia*, and *Resolute* (joined by the *Pawnee* on May 31)—all comprising Commander James H. Ward's Potomac Flotilla—engaged and silenced Confederate batteries at Aquia Creek, Virginia. Ward died in late June when he attempted a landing at Mathias Point. The Potomac Flotilla performed valuable work without the assistance of troops in keeping the river free for Union shipping to the capital, but increasing numbers of Confederate shore batteries rendered this work difficult.

Union forces, meanwhile, began the first of a long series of joint army-navy amphibious operations. If the extensive coastline was a problem for the Union naval forces to blockade, it also was impossible for Confederate forces, already stretched thin facing the Northern armies, to defend. Indeed, the South was obliged to concentrate its defensive efforts along the coasts at a half-dozen key points. Thus, it was relatively easy for Union forces to find places along the Confederate coast to land. The difficulty would come later, when the Union sought to expand coastal enclaves inland and attack the principal Confederate ports.

The first Union amphibious campaign began on August 26, 1861, when Flag Officer Silas H. Stringham departed Hampton Roads with a squadron bound for Hatteras Inlet, North Carolina. It consisted of the *Minnesota*, *Wabash*, *Monticello*, *Pawnee*, Revenue Cutter Service brigantine *Harriet Lane*, tug *Fanny*, and two transports carrying some nine hundred army troops under Maj. Gen. Benjamin F. Butler from Fortress Monroe.

The squadron anchored at Hatteras Inlet the next day. On the 28th, Stringham ordered the bombardment of Confederate Forts Hatteras and Clark and the landing of marines and troops under cover of naval gunfire. The Confederates then abandoned Fort Clark. That evening, under command of Commodore Samuel Barron, two small Confederate gunboats appeared, but they did not interfere with Union operations.

By the 29th, Union forces had secured the inlet. Both Confederate forts surrendered unconditionally. This Union victory was the first real naval triumph of the war, indeed the first Union victory of the war. Securing Hatteras meant that the Union was able to seal off Pimlico Sound from commerce raiding by privateers and blockade runners. This location on the Outer Banks also enabled a base to be established for the Union blockaders and a depot for coal and supplies. This minor Union operation did much to restore morale in the North after the Union defeat in the Battle of Manassas/Bull Run.

In October 1861 the Confederates scored a minor victory against Union ships blockading the mouth of the Mississippi. The operation centered on the ironclad *Manassas*. Built in 1855 as the icebreaker *Enoch Train*, she was purchased in 1859 as a tugboat at New Orleans. On the outbreak of the war, John A. Stevenson raised $100,000 by subscription to convert her into an ironclad ram. The Confederates quickly cut her down and rebuilt her in some secrecy. In place of her upper works the *Manassas* received a convex deck of 12-inch thick oak, covered by 1.5 inches of iron plate. Her bow was filled in solid with timber to make a 20-foot-long ram. The *Manassas* mounted only one gun, a 64-pounder smoothbore, which fired forward through a small bow peephole. To train it, the entire ship was turned. When completed, this first-ever Confederate ironclad was only 387 tons and 134' x 33' in size, 15' longer and 5' wider than her original size. In appearance, apart from a large central smokestack, she resembled a cigar floating on the water.

Stevenson applied for and received on September 12, 1861, a letter of marque as a privateer. Because the *Manassas* was clearly the most powerful vessel available, Confederate Commodore George N. Hollins at New Orleans was reluctant to see her operate independently as a privateer. So, on October 11, Lt. Alexander Warley, acting on Hollins's orders, seized the ironclad and sent Stevenson and his privateer crew ashore. The *Manassas* was then manned by volunteers from the Confederate flotilla. Two months later the Confederate government purchased the ram.

Hollins had no intention of letting his new ship remain idle. The very next night, October 12, accompanied by the armed steamers *Ivy* and *James L. Day*, the ram carried out a surprise attack on Union blockaders off the Head of the Passes on the Mississippi. The Union squadron consisted of the *Richmond*, *Vincennes*, *Water Witch*, *Nightingale*, and *Preble*.

On sighting the blockaders the crew charged the ship's furnaces with tar, tallow, and sulfur to build up maximum pressure as quickly as possible. With only twelve shells aboard, Captain Stevenson of the *Manassas* decided to use only her ram and headed for the Union flagship, screw sloop *Richmond*. The ram struck the sloop hard, holing her below the waterline. Union shot and shell fired against the *Manassas* bounced harmlessly off, but the exchange, especially the collision, damaged the ram. The ironclad's prow was wrenched off, her smokestack carried away, and one of her two engines was dislodged. In this state she had difficulty moving upriver against the current.

The Confederates then sent fire rafts downriver, and the ships of the Union squadron slipped their anchor chains and withdrew toward the sea. In the process both the *Richmond* and the *Vincennes* grounded on the bar. At daylight the ships of the Confederate squadron bombarded the two stranded ships, but the larger and longer range guns aboard the Union squadron held them at bay. The two Union ships were finally under way and left the river, although the crew of the *Richmond* had to throw fourteen of her guns overboard and much shot to do so.

Apart from Charleston, Port Royal in South Carolina—located approximately half way between Savannah and Charleston—was the Confederacy's best natural harbor along the Atlantic coast. The Confederates recognized its importance when they made it one of the first coastal areas to be fortified. Capt. Samuel F. Du Pont, a member of Secretary Welles's strategy board, advised an attack on Hatteras Inlet. The board then suggested an attack on Port Royal.

To maintain an effective blockade the U.S. Navy would need bases close to its area of operations. Port Royal's deep harbor was ideal for this purpose. Du Pont now took charge of the operation, and on October 29, flying his flag on the *Wabash*, he departed Hampton Roads with a considerable force for Port Royal. With seventy-seven vessels, most of them transports and supply vessels, it was the largest U.S. fleet assembled to that point. The ships lifted sixteen thousand men commanded by Brig. Gen. Thomas W. Sherman.

On November 1, as the expedition approached Port Royal, it was hit by a severe storm that scattered the Union ships and jeopardized the entire mission. Damage to the vessels was not extensive, however, and they gradually rendezvoused according to prior instructions. The Union squadron crossed the bar on November 4, and four gunboats—the *Ottawa*, *Seneca*, *Curlew*, and *Pembina*—under Commander John Rodgers Jr. drove off three weaker Confederate gunboats under Flag Officer Josiah Tattnall. The Union gunboats then escorted the transports into the roadstead beyond range of the Confederate forts. Port Royal was well protected by two Confederate earthworks, Forts Beauregard at Bay Point and Fort Walker at Hilton Head, on either side of the harbor entrance. But the two mounted only forty-one guns between them.

The next day, Rodgers conducted a reconnaissance, drawing fire from both forts and in the process determining that they were

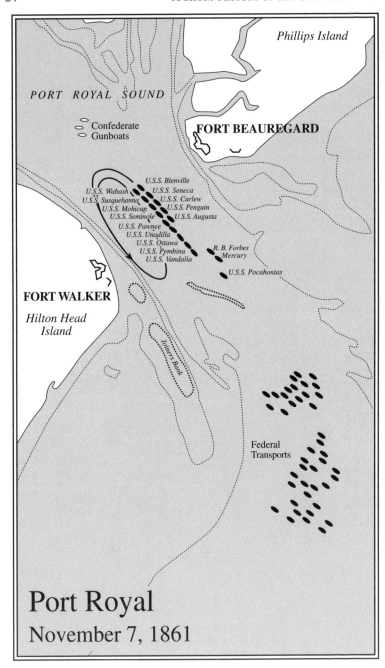

Phillips Island

PORT ROYAL SOUND

Confederate
Gunboats

FORT BEAUREGARD

U.S.S. Bienville
U.S.S. Wabash   *U.S.S. Seneca*
U.S.S. Susquehanna   *U.S.S. Curlew*
U.S.S. Mohican   *U.S.S. Penguin*
U.S.S. Seminole   *U.S.S. Augusta*
U.S.S. Pawnee
U.S.S. Unadilla
U.S.S. Ottawa   *R. B. Forbes*
U.S.S. Pembina   *Mercury*
U.S.S. Vandalia

U.S.S. Pocahontas

FORT WALKER

*Hilton Head
Island*

Joiners Bank

*Federal
Transports*

Port Royal
November 7, 1861

strong. The original plan had been for a joint army-navy attack, but much of the special landing equipment had been lost in the storm. Du Pont decided on a naval attack alone.

By November 7 preparations had been completed for the attack, and at 9:00 A.M. Du Pont led nine warships into Port Royal Sound: the frigate *Wabash* (flag) led, followed by the frigate *Susquehanna*; the sloops *Mohican*, *Seminole*, and *Pawnee*; the gunboats *Unadilla*, *Ottawa*, and *Pembina*; and the sailing sloop *Vandalia* towed by the *Isaac Smith*. The Union ships steamed up midchannel drawing distant fire from both forts until they were well past them; then they reversed course to pass close by Fort Walker. Meanwhile, a Union flanking squadron of gunboats—the *Bienville*, *Seneca*, *Curlew*, *Penguin*, and *Augusta*—interposed itself between the main force and Tattnall's six small Confederate gunboats in the upper harbor.

On the approach to Walker, both sides exchanged heavy fire, the Confederate defenders concentrating on the leading *Wabash*. The Union ships passed within about eight hundred yards of the fort and delivered accurate fire. Steaming against the tide, the larger Union ships were directly in front of the fort for some time. Meanwhile, Du Pont's gunboats took up position to deliver enfilading fire on either flank of Fort Walker. Slowly passing by the fort, Du Pont turned to midchannel and again followed it in while engaging both forts at long range. He then returned to engage Fort Walker, this time at a range of only six hundred yards.

In effect, the Union ships steamed in a great oval to be able to attack both Confederate forts simultaneously. Superior Union firepower soon told as the inexperienced Confederate gunners found it difficult to hit the moving ships. Fire from the Union gunboats enfilading Fort Walker, the more powerful of the two forts, disabled its guns one after another. Commodore Tattnall's Confederate squadron was unable to intervene, although it did rescue some of the defenders from Hilton Head, ferrying them to the mainland.

The great Union swings continued until about 2:00 in the afternoon when the defenders, their ammunition running out, abandoned Fort Walker. All but three of its guns on the waterside had been dismounted or otherwise put out of action. Du Pont had proven that the best defense against an enemy battery is an accurate and high volume of fire. Although the ships had been hit, the Confederate gunners tended to fire high, and most of the damage was aloft and of little consequence. Aboard the fleet only nine men were killed and thirty-seven wounded. After the Confederates left Fort Walker, Du Pont sent ashore a party of marines and seamen under Commander Rodgers. At 2:30 P.M. they hoisted the U.S. flag. An hour later the Confederates abandoned Fort Beauregard. Du Pont then turned over both forts to Sherman.

The Union seizure of Port Royal was important to the blockade because it provided a perfect base for the South Atlantic Blockading Squadron; great stretches of Southern coastline now lay within easy reach of Union gunboats. The Confederates then abandoned their vulnerable coastal positions, withdrawing, except at Charleston and Savannah, beyond the range of Union guns.

Over the next months, Union forces mounted small joint army-navy operations to occupy islands and ports along the entire 150-mile coastal strip from Savannah to Cape Canaveral, Florida. This area was particularly important to the blockaders because it was so close to Bermuda and Nassau, principal ports from which the blockade runners operated. In December the navy made efforts to sink large numbers of sailing ships loaded with stone to block the entrances to these two large coastal seaports. These attempts met with little long-range success. Gradually more and more warships were added to the blockade.

Blockade runners, however, continued to get through. On April 24, 1862, for example, the CSS *Nashville* made it into Wilmington with sixty thousand stand of arms and forty tons of powder. Although penetrating the Union blockade became increasingly difficult, blockade runners supplied the South until the end of the war. The diminished quantity of military goods they brought was sufficient nonetheless to keep the Southern military effort going. How important was this trade? Without the military supplies brought by the blockade runners, the South could not have survived as long as it did. Home production never reached 50 percent of military needs. Blockade runners also brought clothing, chemicals, and medicine. Defeat did not come from lack of materials; the Confederacy simply ran out of manpower.

The year 1862 opened with a series of major naval engagements. In the west in February, Flag Officer Andrew H. Foote, cooperating with troops under Brig. Gen. Ulysses S. Grant, took

Forts Henry and Donelson, while in the east there was a comparable Union victory at Roanoke Island.

Roanoke Island, located at the northern end of Pamlico Sound, North Carolina, controlled passage between Pamlico Sound to the south and Albemarle Sound to the north and west. Federal forces already held Pamlico Sound as a consequence of capturing its main ocean access at Hatteras Inlet. Securing Roanoke Island would give Union forces access to Albemarle Sound with its rivers leading into the interior of North Carolina. Railroad bridges over these rivers ran north to Norfolk, Virginia.

The Union capture of Roanoke Island was a combined arms operation led by Flag Officer Louis M. Goldsborough and Brig. Gen. Ambrose Burnside. Because of the shallow water, the twenty warships under Goldsborough's command were all conversions from tugs, river steamers, and ferry boats. Typical of these was Goldsborough's flagship, the 504-ton *Philadelphia*. An iron-hulled, paddle-wheel steamer, she had operated before the war between Norfolk and Baltimore. Her armament consisted of 2 x 12-pounder rifled boat guns. Commander Stephen C. Rowan in the *Delaware* had command of the fighting ships. The Union warships escorted some fifty transports carrying twelve thousand troops. The Union force left its assembly point at Hatteras Inlet on February 5 but was delayed one day by bad weather.

The Union expedition passed through the narrow channel west of the southern tip of Roanoke Island on the 7th and entered Croatan Sound. To the north of the channel the Confederates had erected a barricade of pilings. Beyond that lay an outgunned squadron of seven gunboats commanded by Flag Officer William F. Lynch. The barricade was covered by Confederate shore batteries on either side of the two-mile-wide channel. A number of Confederate troops also manned Roanoke Island.

At about 10:30 A.M., Rowan's gunboats were joined by seven gunboats belonging to the army. The Union warships then began shelling both the Confederate squadron beyond the barricade and the land batteries on the mainland and Roanoke Island to either side of the channel, especially the earthen works of Fort Barrow at Pork Point. The firing slackened between noon and 2:00 P.M. but then resumed and reached its highest intensity, continuing on until about 5:00 P.M. By about 2:30 two Confederate gunboats, the *Curlew* and *Forrest*, were disabled, but the others continued firing until their ammunition was exhausted. They then steamed about forty miles up Albemarle Sound to Elizabeth City to replenish their supplies. Fort Barrow in particular was hard hit, at times almost hidden by the smoke, sand, and debris thrown up there by Union shot and shell. Rowan's vessels escaped serious injury, thanks to the accuracy of their own fire and by continued maneuvering in the shallow water.

At 3:00 P.M., Union troops went ashore at Ashby's Point on Roanoke Island, their landing covered by naval gunfire. By midnight ten thousand men were ashore, protected in part by a battery of Dahlgren boat howitzers. The next morning both the land attack and the shelling resumed. The Union troops on Roanoke Island, covered by naval gunfire, advanced with little difficulty against the Confederate defenders. At about 4:00 the Confederates surrendered after setting fire to the *Curlew*, mounting one 32-pounder. She blew up.

About the same time, Union ships forced a passage through the obstructions in the shallow channel and were able to steam into Albemarle Sound. Confederate Flag Officer Lynch was unable to do more than offer token, long-range resistance. He withdrew his remaining gunboats up the Pasquotank River. Surprisingly, Union casualties had been light. Although the Union ships had been hit numerous times, the casualties were six killed, seventeen wounded, and two missing.

On February 10, Commander Rowan led thirteen Union gunboats with marines on board up the Pasquotank River to pursue Lynch's gunboats. Badly outnumbered, Lynch manned, and supplied with ammunition, a nearby land battery. After a spirited hour-long engagement, Rowan fought both the shore battery and the gunboats, sinking the *Seabird* and capturing the *Ellis*. Lynch fired the *Black Warrior*, *Fanny*, and *Forrest* to prevent their capture.

During this engagement a Confederate shell hit the *Valley City*. It passed through her magazine and then exploded in a locker that contained fireworks. Her captain, Lt. Commander James C. Chaplain, went to the magazine to help fight the fire. There he discovered Quarter Gunner John Davis seated on an open barrel of powder as the only means of keeping the fire from reaching it.

At the same time, Davis was passing powder to allow the gun division on the upper deck to return fire. For his bravery, in April 1863 he received the Medal of Honor.

Rowan next sent marines ashore to occupy both Elizabeth City and Edenton and to obstruct the Dismal Swamp Canal leading to Norfolk. On March 14, Burnside, supported by Rowan's gunboats, led eleven Federal troops to capture the fortified city of New Bern at the south end of Pamlico Sound on the Neuse River. Soon thereafter Fort Macon, near Beaufort, South Carolina, fell to Union forces.

These victories, coupled with those in the west in which the navy played a leading role, did much to restore morale in the North. The capture of Roanoke Island and attendant operations cut off Norfolk from its main supplies lines and helped bring about its fall three months later, an event that had far-ranging repercussions for the war. The Port Royal operation also secured the North Carolina coast and reduced the amount of Atlantic coastal area under Confederate control to a short stretch from Wilmington, North Carolina, to Charleston, South Carolina, together with the isolated port of Savannah, Georgia.

Chapter Two

The First Clash of Ironclads

THE UNION OBJECTIVE in the east was always to secure the Confederate capital of Richmond. President Lincoln preferred a push directly south that would allow the Union army of the Potomac to protect Washington, but Maj. Gen. George B. McClellan thought he had a better plan. McClellan, who became Union general-in-chief on the retirement of Gen. Winfield Scott in November 1861, planned to take Richmond from the east. Utilizing Union command of the sea, he hoped to outflank Gen. Joseph E. Johnston's defenses by running his army by water down the Chesapeake Bay to Urbanna on the Rappahannock River, only forty-five miles from Richmond, and attack the city from there. Johnston, informed of the plan, countered by withdrawing his forces behind the Rappahannock. McClellan then extended the plan. He would move his forces by water to Fortress Monroe, where they could be supplied by ships. His army then would be moved by detachments up the York and James Rivers. Outflanked, the Confederates would have to withdraw back toward Richmond. As McClellan closed in on the Confederate capital from the east, he would summon Maj. Gen. Irvin McDowell's corps that had been guarding Washington to push south and link up with him to help take Richmond and end the war.

The delay in beginning the campaign, however, allowed the Confederates to block access to the York by constructing defenses at Yorktown. Another Confederate threat loomed on the James in the form of the ironclad ram *Virginia*, which not only could block the James but threaten any Union vessels at Fortress Monroe. In fact, the obstacles were such and the threat so great that, on March 13, Assistant Secretary of the Navy Fox tried to dissuade McClellan from implementing his plan.

It was only natural that the Confederates, who lacked both a navy and the potential to keep up with the North in building warships, would seek ways to offset the Union numerical advantage through technology. One way to do this was through ironclad ships. Mallory saw the importance of the new ironclad ships much more clearly than did his counterpart Wells. On May 10, 1861, Mallory wrote C. M. Conrad, chairman of the congressional Committee on Naval Affairs, a long letter in which he pointed out the ironclad revolution under way in Europe and pushed for an offensive strategy based on ironclads:

> I regard the possession of an iron-armored ship as a matter of the first necessity. Such a vessel at this time could transverse the entire coast of the United States, prevent all blockades, and encounter, with a fair prospect of success, their entire Navy.
>
> If to cope with them upon the sea we follow their example and build wooden ships, we shall have to construct several at one time; for one or two ships would fall an easy prey to her comparatively numerous steam frigates. But inequality of numbers may be compensated by invulnerability; and thus not only does economy but naval success dictate the wisdom and expediency of fighting with iron against wood, without regard to first cost.
>
> Should the committee deem it expedient to begin at once with the construction of such a ship, not a moment is to be lost.[1]

The Confederate Congress agreed with Mallory and promptly appropriated $2 million to purchase or construct ironclads in Europe, but early efforts toward that end were not successful, so Mallory turned to building at least some ironclads at home. On June 10 he directed Lt. John M. Brooke, one of his most talented naval officers, to design an ironclad. Within two weeks Brooke had come up with a plan for a casemated vessel with inclined sides. The plan was finalized on the 23rd at a meeting of Brooke, Mallory, and Naval Constructor John L. Porter and Chief Engineer William P. Williamson from the Gosport Navy Yard. When the planners learned that no engines of the size required were to be found in the Confederacy, Williamson suggested using the engines and boilers on the former U.S. steam frigate *Merrimack* as well as her hull. Brooke and Porter endorsed the plan, and on

July 11, Mallory agreed to convert the *Merrimack* into an ironclad warship.

The *Merrimack* had been at the Gosport Yard on the secession of Virginia. She was to have been moved, but contradictory orders from Washington meant nothing was done. Scuttled in the precipitous Union retreat from the yard, this 3,200-ton vessel, built only in 1856, had been one of the largest and newest warships in the U.S. Navy. Set alight, she had burned only to the waterline, and her hull had largely escaped damage.

Conversion of the *Merrimack* to the *Virginia* illustrated the South's problems with ironclad construction throughout the war. Iron manufacturing capacity was so limited that the navy was forced to rely on iron from militarily nonessential railroad lines, including Richmond's streetcar tracks. But the supply of rail iron was limited, and the navy had to compete with the army for it. Later, at least ten ironclads had to be broken up for lack of iron plate. In 1863 the naval officer charged with construction of the *Albemarle* reported to Secretary Mallory: "It is impossible to obtain any iron unless it is seized. . . . These roads are considered a military necessity and the whole subject of Railroad iron [is] laid before the North Carolina legislature and I am unable to obtain iron."[2] In late 1864, Chief Constructor Porter reported that a dozen vessels were on the stocks awaiting their armor, "but the material is not on hand."[3] The Tredegar Iron Works could cast heavy guns and indeed produced the fine Brooke-designed rifled guns for the *Virginia* and other vessels, and yet it was the only such facility in the South. In 1863 the navy bought and staffed the Selma Foundry Works in Alabama, not only to produce guns but also to roll iron plate, but it never turned out more than one gun per week.

In August 1861 contracts were awarded for construction at Memphis of two ironclads of the *Arkansas*-class: the *Arkansas* and *Tennessee*. A fourth, the *Mississippi*, was to be built at New Orleans. In addition, another ironclad, the *Louisiana*, was laid down at New Orleans. All were quite large ships, designed for seagoing operations. Mallory's strategy was a failure. Of those five vessels, only three—the *Arkansas*, *Louisiana*, and *Virginia*—became operational. The others were destroyed to prevent capture.

Virginia was the first to achieve success. The Confederate raised and rebuilt the *Merrimack*, renaming her the *Virginia*. Porter had charge of the construction, Brooke provided the basic plans for the conversion and had charge of her guns and armor, and Williamson was the chief engineer and oversaw overhaul of her engines. Friction developed between Porter and Brooke (later Porter claimed sole credit for the *Virginia*'s design), but work went forward. Thanks to the dry dock at the naval yard, by mid-July work was well under way in cutting out the burnt portion of the ship. A central casemated structure then was built onto the hull. Armor for this would extend over the hull and into the water. The ironclad was supposed to be ready in November, but the armoring brought delays. As 1-inch plate was inadequate, 2-inch plate was substituted. Beginning in October the Tredegar Iron Works produced the plate, from rolled railroad iron, but rolling the 732 tons of plates for the *Virginia* consumed nearly the entire activity of the Tredegar rolling mills for five months. The last deliveries were not until February 12.

Transporting the plate also proved a problem because of a shortage of rolling stock on the overworked Confederate rail system. In November, Lt. Catesby ap Roger Jones was appointed to expedite this and put together a crew. Despite the fact that fifteen hundred men were working on the ship virtually around the clock, the *Virginia* was not ready for some time. One problem was a dockyard strike in January. That resolved, the plating work was finally completed at the end of the month.

Problems were discovered after the *Virginia* was launched on February 17. Her steering was so sluggish that it took more than one-half hour and four miles to turn 180 degrees. Her engines were unreliable and had been condemned at the end of the *Merrimack*'s last cruise. Even had they been working effectively, the engines were barely adequate for the wooden *Merrimack*; they were totally inadequate for a much heavier ironclad. The *Virginia*'s top speed was only 7 knots. More serious, Porter had miscalculated the *Virginia*'s displacement so she rode too high in the water. Her armor plate was to have extended 2 feet under water, but in places her unarmored wooden hull was submerged only an inch or so. Coal and supplies weighted her down and helped solve the problem, although not completely; it remained a serious concern throughout her career.

The new ship was 263' in length (between perpendiculars, 275' overall) x 51'4" beam x 22' in depth. Her central armored casemate was 160' long, with its sides placed at an angle of 36 degrees from the horizontal. The upper deck of the casemate was a 2-inch-thick iron grating. Both casemate ends were rounded to deflect shot, unique in Confederate ironclads, as was her submerged bow and stern. The upper deck on top of the casemate had three 2-inch-thick iron gratings. Her armor was applied in two layers, the lower running horizontally and the upper vertically. The casemate was pierced by fourteen elliptical gunports: four unevenly spaced on each side and three each at bow and stern.

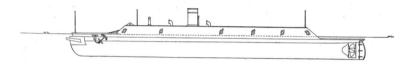

The CSS *Virginia*. *ORN*, series 1, vol. 7 (Washington, DC: Government Printing Office, 1898), 334.

The CSS ironclad *Virginia*. From Alfred H. Guernsey and Henry M. Alden, *Harper's Pictorial History of the Civil War: Contemporary Accounts and Illustrations from the Greatest Magazine of the Time, with 1000 Scenes, Maps, Plans and Portraits* (New York: Harper & Bros., 1866), 251.

The first modern warship to do away completely with rigging, upon completion the *Virginia* mounted ten guns: 6 x 9-inch Dahlgren smoothbores and 2 x 6.4-inch single-banded Brooke rifles in broadsides, and 2 x 7-inch single-banded Brooke rifles in pivot at bow and stern. The ship was supplied with shell for all her guns, but owing to the delays in manufacture and transportation, she had shot for the smoothbores only. The *Virginia* was the prototype for most Confederate ironclads to follow. Ultimately, the South built twenty-one ironclads during the war and laid down twenty-nine more.

The ironclad also had a 1,500-pound iron bow ram or beak about 3 feet long. It was, however, poorly secured to the rest of the ship. The ram seemed a strange throwback in time but was in the forefront of naval thinking. Bearing in mind that the French floating batteries in the Crimean War had been undamaged by Russian shore fire but that ships often sank after collisions with other vessels, a number of naval theorists thought that the ram might replace the gun as the most effective weapon at sea.

Former U.S. Navy officer now Confederate flag officer Franklin Buchanan had charge of all ships in the James. He now took the *Virginia* as his flagship. Buchanan's executive officer, Lieutenant Jones, had charge of fitting out the vessel. The *Virginia* had a crew of 320, included 55 marines. All were largely untrained and most had volunteered from the army. By contrast, virtually all her officers were U.S. Navy veterans.

There was wild and completely unfounded speculation, North as well as South, over the *Virginia*'s capabilities. Secretary Mallory wanted her to steam up the Potomac to Washington and even raid New York City, shelling both cities and destroying their naval yards and shipping. Others thought she might scatter the Union blockading fleet along the Atlantic seaboard.

Such tasks were simply beyond the *Virginia*'s capabilities. Her draft was too deep for her to make it up the Potomac, and it is doubtful she could have gotten across the bar to New York, even with the services of a first-class pilot. She also was not a good sea boat. Buchanan admitted as much to Mallory when he wrote the secretary that in all likelihood she would founder in a gale, or even a heavy swell. Also, her unreliable engines would likely have broken down under the strain of prolonged steaming in a seaway.

At 11:00 A.M., on March 8 the *Virginia* sortied. Most of her crew thought this was a trial run, but Buchanan was determined to take the new warship into action as soon as possible in a surprise effort to destroy the Union blockading fleet and free the Confederate James River Squadron upriver. The *Virginia* thus went into battle without trials or underway training. In fact, Buchanan had planned to attack on the 7th and, had that occurred, he would have had two days to complete destruction of the Union blockaders before the arrival of the *Monitor*. But as fate would have it, a severe storm that also affected the *Monitor* in its passage south forced him to postpone his plans for twenty-four hours.

Hampton Roads, where the resulting engagement was to take place, is simply the large basin into which the James, Nansemond, and Elizabeth Rivers empty before flowing into Chesapeake Bay. The Roads is seven miles across, but the *Virginia*'s deep draft confined her to an area never more than two miles across. The northern shore of the Roads, with Newport News, Hampton, and Fortress Monroe, was occupied by Union troops; the southern, with Norfolk and Portsmouth on the Elizabeth River, by the Confederates. Over the next two days, thousands of soldiers ashore in both armies, as well as civilians, witnessed the battles in the Roads.

Buchanan attempted to interest Maj. Gen. John B. Magruder, commanding Confederate forces between the James and York Rivers in a joint attack on Newport News, but Magruder demurred, whereupon Buchanan vowed to proceed alone. The forces available consisted of the *Virginia* and her 2 small steamer tenders: the *Beaufort* (85 tons and 1 x 32-pounder) and *Raleigh* (65 tons and 2 x 6-pounders), all based in Norfolk. Buchanan also had the three gunboats in Commander John Randolph Tucker's James River Squadron: the former passenger steamers *Patrick Henry* and *Jamestown* each mounted 1 x 10-inch, 1 x 64-pounder, 6 x 8-inch, and 2 x 32-pounder rifled guns; the former tug *Teaser* of only 64 tons had 1 x 32-pounder rifled gun. Facing them in the Roads was an impressive Union force that included 5 big ships with many more guns: the screw frigates *Minnesota* (40) and *Roanoke* (40), the sailing frigates *Congress* (50) and *St. Lawrence* (50), and the razee (cut down) sailing sloop *Cumberland* (24).

Although Union spies had kept Washington well informed about the progress of the *Virginia*, her attack on the morning of

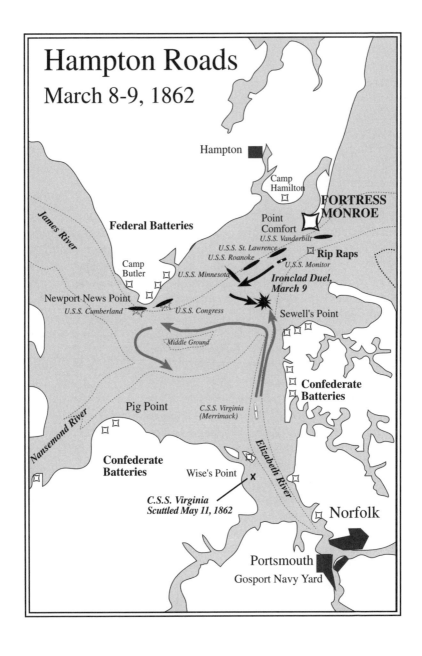

Hampton Roads
March 8-9, 1862

Hampton

Camp
Hamilton

FORTRESS MONROE

James River

Federal Batteries

Point
Comfort

U.S.S. Vanderbilt

U.S.S. St. Lawrence
U.S.S. Roanoke

Rip Raps

Camp
Butler

U.S.S. Monitor

U.S.S. Minnesota

**Ironclad Duel,
March 9**

Newport News Point

U.S.S. Cumberland

U.S.S. Congress

Sewell's Point

Middle Ground

**Confederate
Batteries**

Pig Point

*C.S.S. Virginia
(Merrimack)*

Nansemond River

**Confederate
Batteries**

Wise's Point

Elizabeth River

*C.S.S. Virginia
Scuttled May 11, 1862*

Norfolk

Portsmouth

Gosport Navy Yard

the 8th came as a surprise, with the men aboard the Union ships attending to their normal morning routines. The two nearest ships, the *Cumberland* and *Congress*, were the first likely targets. Given the *Virginia*'s slow speed, once she was spotted their crews had almost an hour to prepare.

The *Beaufort* actually fired the opening shot of the battle, from her single small 32-pounder. Buchanan, meanwhile, made first for the *Cumberland*, which while rated a sloop actually had a heavier battery than the *Congress*. Unfortunately, the tide had moved her athwart the channel with her stern facing the oncoming *Virginia* and her keel in line with her spring anchors. The *Cumberland* could not be turned to deliver a broadside, and only a few of her guns could be brought to bear. The shots bounced off the *Virginia*'s armor. Not so shots from the *Virginia*'s bow pivot gun that immediately wreaked havoc on the *Cumberland*'s starboard quarter. As the *Virginia* came on, the *Congress* let loose a broadside at her, but none of the shot entered open gunports, and the *Virginia*'s response struck home, dismounting a gun, killing or wounding the crew, and starting two fires.

Firing now became general, with such Union ships and shore batteries as were able participating in the fray. After firing several broadsides at the *Cumberland*, Buchanan ordered the *Virginia* to ram. Fearful that his ship, even at 6 knots, might strike so hard that she would become so embedded in the sloop's wooden hull that he would not be able to withdraw, Buchanan at about fifty yards ordered the engines to stop and the *Virginia* simply glided forward on momentum alone.

The *Virginia* struck the Union ship forward at almost a right angle on her starboard side and tore a gaping hole below the waterline. The *Cumberland* began to go down immediately. As she settled by the bow, she almost took the *Virginia* down with her. But when the pressure became too great, the *Virginia*'s ram simply twisted off in the Union ship, and the ironclad's 17-foot propeller managed to pull her away.

This move brought the *Virginia* nearly parallel to the *Congress*, which got off three broadsides at about 100-yard range. Although the iron deflected the shot, two of the *Virginia*'s Dahlgren guns had their muzzles blown off. Both guns continued to fire, but one was so shortened that the muzzle blast set its gunport on fire.

Meanwhile, the *Cumberland* continued to fire into the *Virginia* as she sank. The behavior of the Union crew prompted admiration from the Confederates. Buchanan noted in his formal report to Mallory that "she commenced sinking, gallantly fighting her guns as long as they were above water. She went down with her colors flying."[4]

The *Virginia* then turned to attack the *Congress*, where Franklin Buchanan's brother McKean was paymaster. Although the *Congress* was only several hundred yards away from the *Cumberland*, it took the Confederate ironclad nearly half an hour to come around to be able to attack her.

The *Virginia* was in position about 4:00 P.M. The *Raleigh* and the *Beaufort* did what they could, firing at the *Congress* to keep her occupied. At about this same time, the three vessels in Tucker's James River Squadron also came up, exiting the river and exchanging fire with the Union batteries at Newport News.

While the *Virginia* was gaining position, the commander of the *Congress*, Lt. Joseph B. Smith, had the armed tug *Zouave* tow his ship under the Union batteries at Newport News. This idea was a good one, for with her deep draft the *Virginia* would be unable to ram her. Unfortunately, the tide swung the stern of the *Congress* so that only 2 of her guns could bear on the *Virginia*. Buchanan now took up position about 150 yards off the *Congress*'s stern, and the *Virginia* commenced a deadly raking fire. Within short order, 100 men, some quarter of the Union ship's crew, were casualties. The *Zouave* also came under fire and her rudder was disabled, but a Union gunboat managed to pull her to safety. During this time, the Union shore batteries fired against the *Virginia*, and Buchanan returned fire and silenced several of them. His guns also sank a large transport steamer at the wharf as well as a schooner. Another schooner was captured and sent to Norfolk.

The *Patrick Henry* now joined the *Virginia*, *Beaufort*, and *Raleigh* in shelling the Union frigate. Both of her stern guns were soon disabled and Smith was killed, decapitated by a shell fragment. Still, the frigate sustained nearly an hour of such punishment before she struck. When Smith's father, Commodore Joseph

Smith, learned in Washington that his son's ship had surrendered, he said simply, "Joe's dead."[5]

Buchanan then ordered the *Beaufort* and *Raleigh* to take the officers of the *Congress* prisoner, rescue such wounded as possible, allow the remainder of the crew to escape, and then burn the ship. Lt. William H. Parker of the *Beaufort* took the surrender of the *Congress*, but as the officers were being transferred to the *Beaufort*, a Union regiment ashore opened up with small arms from several hundred yards away, hitting foe and friend alike. Parker was among those wounded, and he soon ordered the *Beaufort* to cast off and move to safety with many wounded aboard. He did not first tell Buchanan, who watched in vain for the telltale smoke that would show that the frigate was on fire.

Soon it was apparent to Buchanan that Parker had been driven off by hostile fire. Furious over what he considered a breach of the laws of the sea, Buchanan conveniently ignored the fact that the fire had come from troops ashore who certainly had not surrendered. His flag lieutenant, Robert Minor, then volunteered to take a boat and do the job. Minor set out with eight men in one of the *Virginia*'s boats but, despite a white flag, also came under fire. With Minor and several others of his party wounded, the boat returned to the ironclad. Buchanan was livid, believing the fire was coming from the *Congress*, but that was not true. He insisted that the *Congress* be destroyed. The *Virginia*'s gunners then set to work, firing into the frigate and setting her alight with hot shot heated in the ironclad's boilers. The few survivors on the Union ship leaped into the water and swam for shore.

Buchanan then foolishly seized a musket and went to the top of the casemate and began firing at the troops on shore, aiming particularly at the officers who he believed were responsible for this "breach" of the rules of war. The Union troops fired back, and soon Buchanan, wounded in the thigh by a musket ball, slumped to the deck. Buchanan was then carried below. His wound, feared fatal, turned out not to be life threatening, but Buchanan was forced to transfer command to Jones. In the charges and countercharges after the event concerning accusations of dishonorable behavior, the Union side quite naturally pointed out that the fire had come from the troops ashore, that the *Beaufort* was a legitimate target, and that the *Congress* was flying a white flag, actually two of them, when Buchanan ordered fire renewed against the ship.

Sometime after 5:00, with the *Congress* in flames and Jones in command, the *Virginia* lobbed a few shells at the Union flagship *Minnesota*, which in an effort to escape had run aground. But the *Virginia*'s pilots argued that the ship must return to her base before dark or risk running aground. The ironclad's engines were also laboring, and her crew was exhausted from the long day. Jones decided to retire, confident he would complete the destruction of the other Union vessels the next day. The *Virginia* fired a few long-range broadsides at the *St. Lawrence* and then returned to her base.

Despite his wound, Buchanan had reason to be pleased. His ship had destroyed 2 major Union combatants with a cost of 250 dead and 75 wounded. Another 26 were captured. Confederate losses had been slight. Only the *Virginia* suffered visible damage. Hit more than 100 times, her casemate had been swept clean of boats, davits, railings, and the like. Her smokestack was punctured in many places, she was leaking at the bow, and 2 of her guns had been damaged. Some of her armor plates were loosened and her ram was gone. Two men were dead and 8 others wounded.

That night, as the *Congress* went up in a fiery spectacle, workers and the crew of the *Virginia* carried out what repairs they could, confident they would be sufficient to complete their work of destruction the next day. At the same time, a strange craft put into the Roads, visible by the light of the burning *Congress*. She was the Union ironclad *Monitor*. Designed and built by John Ericsson, she was ready for battle not a moment too soon.

Washington was well aware of the construction of the *Virginia*. Thus, in August 1861, the U.S. Congress appropriated $1.5 million for ironclad construction and authorized a special board of naval officers to examine proposals and make recommendations on those to be built. Welles appointed three senior officers to the Ironclad Board: Commodore Hiram Paulding and Commander Charles H. Davis, with Commodore Joseph Smith as chairman. The board wanted light-draft vessels capable of operating off the Southern coasts. Sixteen proposals were received, and in September the board recommended construction of three experimental ironclads: the *Monitor*, *Galena*, and *New Ironsides*.

The *Monitor* was the first completed. Designer Ericsson had experienced problems with the Federal government over the construction of USS *Princeton* in the 1840s, and he had vowed never to undertake another government contract. Nonetheless, he offered his services to the government. The Ironclad Board initially rejected Ericsson's unorthodox proposal but changed its decision after a masterful presentation by the designer in person.

In contrast to the lengthy delays in building the *Virginia*, the *Monitor* was to be completed in record time; the contract, signed in October, required what some called "Ericsson's Folly" to be completed in one hundred days, by January 12. The ship was laid down on October 25. Even the tireless Ericsson was not able to meet the deadline, but the ship was completed and ready for trials by February 19. The contract was one of the most unusual in history. Because his warship was so revolutionary, Ericsson and his partners had to assume all the risk themselves. The contract specified that if the ship failed in any way, with the navy to determine what constituted failure, all money advanced for the construction would be refunded to the government. The board had, in fact, accepted Ericsson's design only because of the threat posed by the *Virginia* and because Ericsson promised delivery so quickly.

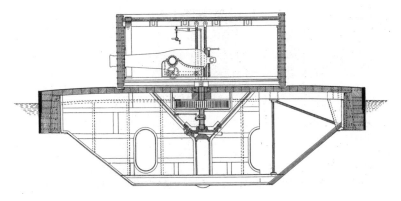

Transverse section through turret of the original monitor. *ORN*, series 1, vol. 7 (Washington, DC: Government Printing Office, 1898), 24.

Conversion of the *Virginia* had begun two months before the keel of the *Monitor* had been laid. The *Monitor* was commissioned on February 25, 1862. The new ship revolutionized naval warfare.

Entirely of iron, she incorporated many innovations, including forced draft ventilation of her interior. She was built without rigging or sails; Ericsson simply ignored that requirement in the contract. Only 987 tons' displacement, she was 179' long x 41' 6" beam, with a draft of only 10' 6". Her 2 engines delivered 320 horsepower to her one screw. The design speed was 9 knots, but the actual speed was slightly less. Her crew complement was small, only 10 officers and 48 men. The *Monitor* in effect had 2 hulls. The upper or armored raft was supported by a lower iron hull. The raft portion was armored with 2 inches of iron on her deck and 4.5 inches of iron on the sides, extending to shield the hull to a depth of 3' 6" below the waterline. The *Monitor*'s most visible part was a 9-foot-tall turret amidships weighing 120 tons. Pierced by 2 gunports, it mounted side by side a pair of 11-inch smoothbore Dahlgren guns. The turret and a small pilothouse forward (only 3' 10" above the deck) were protected by 8 and 9 inches of iron, respectively. With the interior diameter of the turret something less than 20 feet, it was quite cramped once the guns and crews were in place.

The *Monitor* had very slight freeboard (only 18 inches) and, with her turret the principal visible part, she came to be called "a hat on the water" or "cheesebox on a raft." Most of her machinery was below the waterline with only the turret and small pilothouse forward as targets. Her revolving spindle-type turret, the first use of a turret in actual warfare, enabled her gunports to be masked from enemy fire while her guns were being reloaded.

The heavy weight of early turrets precluded their use high in the ship, and for that reason Ericsson designed the *Monitor*, and other monitors to follow, with very low freeboard. The other difficulty with the turreted warship was the inefficiency of early steam propulsion that meant sails were still required, but a sail rig was largely impractical on a turreted monitor. As a consequence, the early monitors were in effect coastal vessels and not seagoing ships. They were particularly unsuited for the U.S. Navy's primary duty of the blockade, for in rough seas the crews had no choice but to batten down hatches and remain below.

Lt. John L. Worden received command of the new ship. He confessed his hope of becoming a hero, but the Civil War began badly for him. Captured by the Confederates in April 1861 while returning overland from Pensacola, he had served seven months in prison before being exchanged, and he had only recently recovered his health. Worden commanded a mixed crew of regulars and wartime volunteers. But all those aboard were volunteers; the navy had been reluctant to assign anyone to such an untried vessel. Ordered to Hampton Roads on March 4, the *Monitor*'s departure was delayed by a storm. Only on the 6th did Worden believe it safe to leave the Brooklyn Navy Yard.

The *Monitor* proceeded south under tow by the steam tug *Seth Low* and propelled by her own engines. Two other warships accompanied them: the steam gunboats *Currituck* and *Sachem*. Never designed as an oceangoing vessel and in any case suffering the problems associated with any brand-new weapon, the *Monitor* nearly sank in her passage south.

The first day passed uneventfully, but after midnight a storm came up and grew increasingly stronger, starting leaks. It also revealed a dreadful error on the part of workers at the Brooklyn Navy Yard. Ericsson had designed the turret to fit snugly with its own great weight to serve as a seal against the admission of water. On their own, the workers had jacked up the turret and inserted a gasket of oakum—bits of old rope—around the entire base to act as a seal. The storm dislodged bits of this gasket, creating what became a 63-foot circumferential opening through which the sea now poured. With the pumps unable to keep up with the influx of water, the ship was in danger of going down.

There were other problems, including water rushing in through the observation slits in the little pilothouse forward and through air intake vents on the deck. The latter stretched belts on the blower fans, which stopped. The engines then halted, and carbon dioxide began to spread through the ship.

In desperation, Worden organized a bucket brigade. The work also served to calm the men. Finally, after some five hours the *Seth Low* succeeded in towing the *Monitor* into calmer water near shore, and the crew was able to repair the blower belts and clear out the carbon dioxide and then restart the boilers and engines. Slowly, the pumps began to clear the water.

The second evening passed quietly, but shortly after midnight the ship was again in peril when the sea became rough. The same crewmen at the Brooklyn Navy Yard who had inserted the oakum also had ignored Ericsson's instructions to plug the hawser pipe through which the anchor chain passed. Seawater now poured through it in a great stream, and the blowers were again in danger of stopping. Then the pitching of the ship caused the wheel ropes to jump off the steering wheel and become jammed. Once again the *Seth Low* was able to tow the ship to calmer waters and the danger passed.

Finally, at about 3:00 P.M. on the 8th, the crew sighted Cape Henry, the southern part of the entrance to Chesapeake Bay. They were then some fifteen miles from their destination. As they approached they could hear the boom of cannon and see the smoke of exploding shells. When a pilot came aboard, he confirmed to the officers that the *Virginia* had sortied and was in the process of destroying the Union fleet, ship by ship.

Worden came alongside the *Roanoke* at about 9:00 P.M. and conferred with Capt. John Marston. Reports that the *Virginia* was almost ready had led Welles to order Marston to have the *Monitor* proceed directly to Washington to protect the capital should the *Virginia* attempt to go up the Potomac. Marston chose to disregard Welles's instructions and ordered Worden to defend the *Minnesota*. At about 1:00 A.M. on the 9th, the *Monitor* anchored alongside the frigate. Shortly thereafter, the fire on the *Cumberland* reached her magazine, and she blew up with a great roar. Few men aboard the *Monitor* slept that night.

Early the next morning, March 9, the *Virginia* steamed out. Jones could see what remained of the *Congress* still burning; beyond her lay the *Minnesota*, still grounded and, further on toward Fortress Monroe, the *St. Lawrence* and the *Roanoke*. Both these ships had grounded while under the tow of tugs but had been pulled free and taken where they could be covered by the guns of Fortress Monroe. The *Minnesota* appeared easy prey. The sea was calm and the day clear, and Jones ordered the *Virginia* to make for the Union flagship.

Aboard the *Monitor*, Worden and his officers were on top of the turret, training their glasses to search for their opponent. At about 7:30 they saw the *Virginia* slip her moorings and, with her consorts the *Patrick Henry*, *Jamestown*, and *Teaser*, steam out into the main channel for Fortress Monroe and then turn and head for the *Minnesota*. Black smoke belched from her damaged funnel.

Worden ordered the *Monitor* to prepare for battle. The men were exhausted. Many had not slept for the past forty-eight hours, and they had had little to eat. Their ship, at least, was ready.

As the *Virginia* steamed for the *Minnesota*, the crew of the Confederate ironclad could see a strange craft move away from the side of the Union frigate. She was the strangest vessel any of them had ever seen and seemed insignificant indeed. A midshipman on the *Virginia* thought it might be a raft carrying one of the *Minnesota*'s boilers for repairs.

Worden positioned the *Monitor* in front of the *Minnesota*. The Union ship was far more maneuverable than her opponent, but she was only a fraction of the *Virginia*'s size and mounted but two guns. There were serious doubts on the Union side that she would prove a worthy opponent for the *Virginia*.

Jones, at least, knew what the *Monitor* was, but he wanted to ignore her until he had finished off the *Minnesota*. When about a mile from the grounded frigate, he ordered his ship to commence fire and almost immediately a round from the forward 7-inch Brooke rifle hit the frigate, starting a fire. A stern gun on the *Minnesota* replied, but the shot ricocheted off the *Virginia*'s armor.

Worden intended to protect the flagship to the best of his ability, and he ordered the *Monitor* to make straight for the *Virginia* but to hold fire until he gave the order. Worden occupied the pilothouse; his executive officer, Lt. Samuel Dana Greene, had charge of the turret and directed the ship's gunnery. Ericsson had installed a speaking tube between the two for conversation, but it broke, and several members of the crew carried communications back and forth.

Shells passed back and forth to and from the *Minnesota* and *Virginia* until the *Monitor* had closed the range. As the *Monitor*'s guns could not fire directly forward because of the pilothouse, Worden ordered the ship to turn parallel to the *Virginia* and ordered, "Commence firing!"

The two ironclads began their battle, which lasted three and one-half hours, until noon. The *Virginia*'s consorts were only spectators to the struggle. The *Monitor*'s heavy guns would have made short work of them. The battle was fought at very close range, from a few yards to about two hundred; and both warships were constantly in circling motion, although at one point the *Virginia* grounded and it was some time before she was able to get free. With his ship still grounded, Jones came down from the spar deck to see the men standing by their guns. He turned to the officer in charge and demanded to know why the guns were not being fired. Lt. John R. Eggleston responded: "Why, our powder is very precious, and after two hours' incessant fire I find that I can do her about as much damage by snapping my thumb at her every two minutes and a half."[6]

Seeing that his own fire was having no effect on his opponent, Jones decided to ram the *Monitor*. Even with the loss of her ram, he believed that the weight of the *Virginia* would drive the *Monitor* under. He explained to the officers that he intended to ram the *Monitor* and then board her. But as one of the *Virginia*'s junior officers noted, "The Ship was as unwieldy as Noah's ark."[7]

After an hour of maneuvering, Jones thought he saw his chance and ordered his ship ahead, full steam. But the more nimble *Monitor* turned aside and received only a glancing blow. The crew of the *Monitor* was ready for any boarding attempt. Should that occur, they planned to toss out hand grenades from the gunports.

Meanwhile, Worden tried to concentrate the *Monitor*'s gunfire on his antagonist's vulnerable propeller and rudder. He also attempted to ram that area, but the try resulted in a near miss. Worden did have to disengage after about two hours of combat, however, to resupply with ammunition. Jones seized the opportunity to try to sink the *Minnesota*, but shoal water halted him almost a mile away. Still, the *Virginia*'s guns did inflict some damage on the frigate and also disabled a tug trying to tow her to safety. The *Monitor* then returned, and the struggle between the two ironclads was renewed.

The poorly drilled crew of the *Monitor* was able to fire her guns only about every seven or eight minutes, but her rotating turret meant her guns were a target only when they were about to fire. The *Virginia*, however, sustained damage from twenty hits from the forty-one 180-pound shells fired by the *Monitor*. In places the wooden backing behind the armor plate cracked and splintered. Although the more numerous Confederate guns fired more often, most of the *Virginia*'s shots went high. Those that hit did little damage. The *Monitor* was struck but twenty-four times and, although the concussion of a shell hitting the turret knocked down people inside, the shells only dented the armor.

A few minutes after noon, Worden was stunned and temporarily blinded by a direct hit to the pilothouse's observation slit. He ordered the *Monitor* to sheer off to assess damage, and she drifted away from the battle in the direction of Fortress Monroe. By the time Executive Officer Greene, just twenty-two years old and a lieutenant for only a year, had taken command, the two ships were nearly a mile apart.

The shell that wounded Worden was a fortunate hit, for it was at this point that the *Virginia* went aground. But for the confusion and delay of some twenty to thirty minutes during the change of command aboard the *Monitor*, she could have shelled a stationary target, probably with devastating effect. Her boiler safety valves tied shut, the *Virginia* eventually freed herself.

When the *Monitor* at last returned, Greene saw the *Virginia* withdrawing. Jones had decided to return to Norfolk for repairs. Greene declined to pursue, claiming his orders were to act on the defensive and protect the *Minnesota*. It was a strange set of circumstances in which each side interpreted the actions of the other as meaning its opponent was beaten.

The inconclusive battle was in effect a draw. The *Virginia* had suffered some cracked plates and was leaking; the *Monitor* was virtually unscathed. No one had been killed, and Worden was the only one seriously wounded. The battle might have turned out differently had the *Virginia* concentrated her fire on the *Monitor*'s pilothouse, a difficult target in the best of conditions, or if she had fired solid shot instead of shell, the type of projectile best suited against the wooden warships that she had expected to engage at Hampton Roads. On the other hand, the *Monitor*'s fire should have been directed at her opponent's waterline where the shells were most likely to have effect; her 11-inch guns easily could have employed powder charges of thirty pounds instead of the fifteen pounds decreed. The reduced charge was a consequence of the explosion of the 12-inch wrought-iron "Peacemaker" gun aboard the *Princeton* in 1844 that had killed the secretary of state, secretary of the navy, and six others. The navy reacted by decreeing that no gun could be fired with a powder charge more than half that for which it had been designed. This mistaken order was revoked after the *Monitor–Virginia* engagement. Had this been done beforehand, the battle's outcome probably would have been different.

Worden got his wish and became a hero, with President Lincoln visiting him at his bedside. Although he remained blind in one eye and experienced physical pain the rest of his life, Worden recovered sight in the other eye and returned to duty late in the year. He finished his naval service as a rear admiral.

The battle between the two vessels was not renewed, but in balance it was a strategic victory for the North, for the Union blockade remained in force. Mallory's hope that the *Virginia* might break the blockade proved illusory. Her deep draft and lack of seaworthiness precluded that. Repaired, she did reenter Hampton Roads on two occasions, but the *Monitor*'s orders to remain on the defensive prevented a new engagement. Merely by surviving, the *Monitor* assured the safety of the Union transports and supply ships and, hence, continuation of McClellan's peninsula campaign. As long as she remained afloat and in position, however, the *Virginia* defended the Norfolk area and was a barrier to Union forces going up the James.

The engagement signaled a new era in naval warfare: ironclad vessels had fought one another for the first time. The era of the metal ship had already arrived, but the *Monitor–Virginia* clash gave emphasis to the revolution in progress. As Capt. John Dahlgren summed up, "Now comes the reign of iron—and cased sloops are to take the place of wooden ships."[8] The London *Times* remarked that the Royal Navy suddenly had dropped from having 149 first-class warships to just 2—its own ironclads. The editors opined that apart from the ironclads *Warrior* and *Ironside*, there was not a single ship "that it would not be madness to trust to an engagement with that little *Monitor*."[9]

The battle certainly awakened opinion in the North on the value of sea power, and it renewed the confidence of leaders on both sides that the future of naval warfare lay with ironclads. Each type proved a model for such construction on that particular side. However, both vessels did not long survive. McClellan planned to proceed up the peninsula to Richmond and to use the navy to carry troops up the James and York Rivers to outflank the Confederate defenders. On March 17, when the Navy Department had positive information that McClellan indeed planned to start the great movement down the Chesapeake Bay, Welles rushed every possible vessel to Hampton Roads to participate, including some chartered vessels to be used as rams against the *Virginia*, should that prove necessary. One of the steamers assembled for this purpose was the *Vanderbilt*. Donated by Cornelius Vanderbilt, she cruised later for Confederate raiders on the high seas.

The Union troops were ashore by April 4, but they advanced against unexpectedly strong Confederate positions placed across the peninsula from Yorktown in the north to the James River west of Newport News in the south. McClellan, who became known as the "Virginia Creeper" for his glacial speed, stalled before Yorktown. On April 5 he began its siege. McClellan kept urging Flag Officer Goldsborough to either attack the Confederate works at Yorktown or to run past them, but Goldsborough refused to weaken his forces at Hampton Roads, apart from detaching several gunboats to shell Yorktown's defenses, which they did intermittently until the Confederates evacuated.

Goldsborough's caution seemed justified when on April 11, the *Virginia*, under Flag Officer Josiah Tattnall, made an appearance in Hampton Roads with five smaller steamers. The Confederates captured three smaller Union sailing ships off Hampton before returning to their base on the Elizabeth River. Goldsborough refused the challenge but kept his own ships near Fortress Monroe and the fortifications opposite it at the Rip Raps to cover the army's base and its essential water lines of communication east and north.

Goldsborough was confident he could turn back any Confederate thrust. His defense centered on the *Monitor*, but he also had the steamer rams and many large guns ashore. At the same time, Goldsborough was reluctant to initiate offensive operations by sending the *Monitor* out after the *Virginia*. Doing so would mean that the other support would not be available, and the loss of the ironclad might spell disaster for the rest of the Union squadron.

Confederate naval commander Tatnall followed a similar line of reasoning. Merely preserving the *Virginia* acted as a break on McClellan's movement up the James. Thus, on April 11, Tattnall was satisfied merely to throw a few long-range shots in the *Monitor*'s direction before retiring.

Union fears over the *Virginia* were lessened on April 24, when the *Monitor* received company at Hampton Roads in the form of the ironclad *Galena*. This second of the experimental ironclads had been designed by Samuel H. Pook. She was 210' x 16' 11" in size and 950 tons' displacement. Commissioned in April, she was armed with 4 x 9-inch Dahlgren smoothbores and 2 x 100-pounder Parrott rifles. Equipped with a two-mast schooner rig to supplement her single-screw propeller, the *Galena* had 3.25-inch side armor of interlocking iron bars. Disappointing as a ship type, her armor proved susceptible to plunging fire striking at almost straight angles against her tumblehome sides.

Meanwhile, the Federals stalled before Yorktown. Confederate Major General Magruder with only fifteen thousand men won a much needed delay. Magruder, who loved theatricals, hoodwinked McClellan, who had seven times his number of troops, into believing that he faced many more Confederates. The siege went on for a month, the Confederates not evacuating Yorktown until May 3 and Union forces occupying it the next day. Union Commander William Smith in the *Wachusett* then reconnoitered the mouth of the York, proceeding up for a distance and raising the Union flag at Gloucester Point across the river from Yorktown.

A stubborn rear-guard action at Williamsburg on May 5 prevented McClellan from coming into contact with the main portion of General Johnston's army. On May 6–7, Smith took the *Wachusett*, *Chocura*, and *Sebago* to escort Union transports up the York to West Point. The Union gunboats covered the landing by troops and countered Confederate shore fire contesting the landing. Smith also sent another of his gunboats, the *Currituck*, up the Pamunkey, a tributary of the York. She captured two Confederate schooners and reported the destruction of others.

On May 8 the *Monitor*, supported by the *Dacotah*, *Naugatuck*, *Seminole*, and *Susquehanna*, shelled Confederate batteries at Sewell's Point, principally to explore the possibilities of landing troops to move against Norfolk. That same day a tug deserted Norfolk, with the men aboard bringing news that a Confederate evacuation was under way and that the *Virginia* would soon steam up the James in the company of Confederate gunboats. Goldsborough hoped that when the Confederate ironclad sortied, he could draw her into deep water, providing an opportunity for his high-speed steamers to ram. Lincoln, acting as commander-in-chief of Union forces at Hampton Roads, wrote to Goldsborough saying that if he could contain the *Virginia* without them, he should send the *Galena* and two gunboats up the James at once to support McClellan. Goldsborough did so, and this action silenced two Confederate shore batteries and forced the Confederate gunboats *Jamestown* and *Patrick Henry* to return up the James.

On May 10 the Confederates set fire to the Norfolk Navy Yard before evacuating. Union troops then crossed Hampton Roads from Fortress Monroe, landing at Ocean View and occupying Norfolk just after the departing Confederates. That same day the Confederates also evacuated Pensacola, Florida. The *Virginia* departed Norfolk on the 10th. Tattnall hoped to get her up the James and was assured by river pilots that the ironclad could reach within forty miles of Richmond, if she was lightened to 18' draft. The crew had worked most of the night to lighten her as much as possible, but the pilots said it would be impossible to get above Jamestown because of low water from a prevailing western wind. Tattnall now had a dilemma. His ship had been lightened to the point where she could no longer be safely fought. The armor barely protected the waterline when she was fully loaded, and now her wooden hull was exposed.

When the *Virginia* sortied on May 11, she was not in water deep enough for Goldsborough's steamers to ram. Instead, Lt. John Taylor Wood ran the *Virginia* aground near Craney Island and burned her to keep her from falling into Union hands. Much of her crew, including gunners, then proceeded to Drewry's Bluff (property owned by Augustus H. Drewry) to man new batteries there.

The destruction of the *Virginia* had a tremendous impact on the peninsula campaign. It not only removed the only Confederate threat to the Union base at Fortress Monroe but also gave Goldsborough the run of the James. His ships now had free passage up the river as far as Drewry's Bluff, which might have saved the Union campaign from possible disaster.

On May 8, meanwhile, Commander John Rodgers in the *Galena* proceeded up the James. He engaged two Confederate shore batteries and in the process grounded at Hog Island and remained stuck for thirty-six hours. Finally, the *Galena* got free and continued up the river. By the 11th she was as far as Upper Brandon. There was no sign of the Federal troops, however; they were only leisurely pursuing the retreating Confederates toward Richmond. Because there were still five Confederate gunboats in the river and the *Virginia* had been destroyed, Goldsborough reinforced Rodgers by sending him the *Monitor* and *Naugatuck*. The latter, built by John Stevens, had been used as an experimental vessel. Taken into the navy from the Revenue Service, she was fitted out as a twin-screw ironclad to demonstrate Stevens's grand design of the "Stevens Battery." Her innovations included a system for flooding the forward and aft compartments to partially submerge the hull during battle, making her less vulnerable to enemy fire.

Rather unrealistically, Goldsborough now ordered the Union ships to proceed to Richmond and shell the city until it surrendered. The Confederate capital, he hoped, would fall to a naval coup de main. Unsupported, the Union ships nonetheless made it up the James to Drewry's Bluff, perhaps seven miles from the Confederate capital.

At 6:30 A.M. on the 15th, Commander Rodgers's James River Squadron, broken off from the North Atlantic Blockading Squadron, and consisting of the *Galena* (flag), *Monitor*, *Naugatuck*, and wooden gunboats *Aroostook* and *Port Royal*, came in sight of Confederate defenses located at Drewry's Bluff. This was the best, and the last, place to stop a Union advance upriver against Richmond. The site had been officially designated Fort Darling but continued to be known simply as Drewry's Bluff. Little work had been carried out there because the Confederates presumed the *Virginia* would stop any Union attempt up the James. Begun in March, work on the fortifications intensified after the fall of Yorktown.

At Drewry's Bluff there was a sharp bend in the James where it narrowed with high, sheer 90-foot cliffs along the south bank of the river. After the digging of gun emplacements, Gen. Robert E. Lee's oldest son, Brig. Gen. G. W. C. Lee, supervised installation of a battery of three heavy guns at the top of the bluffs. The defenders also sank hulks in the river and used pile drivers to position cribs of stone and other debris. Tucker, commander of the James River

Squadron, knew that his wooden ships were no match for the more powerful Union ironclads, so he decided to sacrifice one of his two most powerful ships, sinking the *Jamestown* as an added river obstruction.

The Confederate battery in the fort was reinforced by the addition of five guns from Tucker's squadron, positioned outside the works. The defenders thus had a total of only eight guns: four rifled and four smoothbore. Appropriately enough, Augustus Drewry commanded the battery as captain of the Southside Heavy Artillery. Also present were crewmen of the *Virginia* under Lieutenant Jones, determined to have another go at the *Monitor*, and a detachment of Confederate marines. As positioned, the defenders' guns commanded a one-mile stretch of the river downstream.

Robert E. Lee, exceeding his military authority as advisor to President Davis, detached a brigade of infantry, so marksmen in rifle pits also lined the riverbank. Finally, the Confederate gunboat *Patrick Henry* took up position behind the obstructions to add her 8-inch smoothbore cannon to the defense. Navy Commander Ebenezer Ferrand had overall command. Because the Confederate preparations had been so hasty, there was no way of knowing whether they would be sufficient to stop Union naval action.

The James was too narrow at this point for the Union ships to maneuver, and the obstructions easily blocked the deeper draft ironclads. Before their crews could hope to work at removing the obstructions, the shore battery would have to be neutralized. Rodgers did not hesitate to attempt this feat, the first big test for the flagship *Galena*.

At 7:45, Rodgers boldly positioned the *Galena* about six hundred yards from the bluff and anchored broadside to the channel so that her guns could be brought to bear. Even before the flagship was in position, however, the Confederate defenders sent two shots crashing into her port bow. In the subsequent exchange of fire (known as the First Battle of Drewry's Bluff), the *Galena* bore the brunt of the battle. The *Monitor* passed by her and endeavored to join in but found her guns could not be elevated sufficiently to fire on the Confederate batteries along the bluff. She retired and remained at longer range with the wooden screw gunboat *Aroostook* and side-wheeler *Port Royal*. The Confederate gunners then concentrated on the *Galena*.

The nearly three-and-one-half-hour-long battle, fought from about 7:45 to 11:00, saw perhaps one hundred shots fired by the Confederate side and half that number from the Union ships. The result was certainly unsatisfactory from the Federal standpoint. The *Galena* fought virtually alone. The *Naugatuck* was out of action halfway through the battle when her 6.4-inch (100-pounder) Parrott rifle burst, and the *Port Royal* was kept busy firing into the woods along the riverbank against Confederate troops there. Her captain was wounded by a sharpshooter.

The *Galena* took a terrible pounding from the Confederate heavy guns, revealing the serious shortcomings in her armor arrangement. She was struck forty-three times; thirteen of the shots penetrated, one embedding itself in the opposite side of the hull. Her timbers and frames were cut up, she was briefly on fire, and she was taking on water. Personnel casualties numbered thirteen killed and eleven wounded. Cited for his role in the action, Cpl. John B. Mackie of the *Galena* was subsequently awarded the first Medal of Honor to a member of the U.S. Marine Corps.

Yet Rodgers withdrew only when his crew had expended most of the ship's ammunition. Afterward he noted with considerable understatement and a bit of sarcasm that the engagement had proved the *Galena* was not shot-proof. In the exchange the Confederates had lost only seven killed and eight wounded.

Rodgers claimed that had troops been available to be landed, Drewry's Bluff would have been taken. Had this occurred, the campaign against Richmond might have worked out differently. Drewry's Bluff was the last defense on the river before Richmond; thus, the Confederate stand there might have saved the capital. After the rebuff at Drewry's Bluff, Rodgers fell back downriver to City Point where he could keep the James and Chickahominy Rivers under observation. He remained there until late June.

Later, the Confederates strengthened the Drewry's Bluff defenses and established their naval academy there. By the end of 1862, moreover, they added another ironclad on the James: the *Richmond*. In 1864 two other ironclads, the *Fredericksburg* and *Virginia II*, joined the James River Squadron. All three were destroyed at Richmond upon the Confederate evacuation of the capital, April 3, 1865. In addition to the ironclads, the Confederates deployed an elaborate system of electrically detonated mines, developed by Matthew F. Maury.

The day before the battle at Drewry's Bluff, the Army of the Potomac had reached its advance base on the Pamunkey River twenty miles from Richmond. Despite overwhelming strength, McClellan stopped to await reinforcement by McDowell's corps. The main Union base was at White House on the Pamunkey, in close proximity to the York River. On the 17th, on McClellan's request, the gunboats *Sebago* and *Currituck* raided up the Pamunkey, some twenty-five miles beyond White House. Later the *Cuttick* and *Corwin* conducted a similar foray up the Mattapony River, paralleling the Pamunkey.

McClellan moved the bulk of his forces across the Chickahominy River, which then extended in a great vee, the upper arm of which stretched out to meet McDowell, the lower reached out to within five miles of Richmond, just beyond Fair Oaks Station. On May 31, General Johnston attacked two Union corps on the south bank and isolated by the flooded river from the main part of McClellan's army. Only the timely arrival of another corps that had managed to cross the river prevented a disastrous Union defeat. In what became known as the Battle of Seven Pines, both sides sustained heavy losses, including Johnston, who was severely wounded. On June 1, Robert E. Lee assumed command of the Army of Northern Virginia.

In an offensive move to drive McClellan off the peninsula, Lee sent forces under Maj. Gen. Thomas J. "Stonewall" Jackson to attack the vulnerable Union right flank while he himself struck McClellan's center. Alerted by a cavalry raid, McClellan withdrew to the protection of Union gunboats on the James River. In what became known as the Seven Days' Battles, on June 26, Lee struck the extreme Union right at Mechanicsville and for six days attacked the smaller Union forces. But McClellan inflicted heavy losses on the Confederates while he withdrew across the Chickahominy. In response to appeals from McClellan, on the 29th, Rodgers took the *Galena*, *Monitor*, *Aroostook*, and *Mahaska* up the James from City Point, leaving three other gunboats to safeguard the army supply ships. He sent three other gunboats, the *Jacob Bell*, *Delaware*, and *Satellite*, up the Chickahominy.

At Malvern Hill on July 1, the withdrawing Army of the Potomac withstood Lee's desperate attacks. The Union gunboats in the river, including the much-maligned *Galena*, played a key role with their heavy guns, helping to cover the Union withdrawal and perhaps preventing disaster. On July 2 the Union forces ashore established a new position at Harrison's Landing, across the river from City Point, chosen because it lent itself to protection on both flanks by the gunboats. McClellan himself, aboard the *Galena*, had helped pick out the position.

On July 2 the Confederates disengaged; the peninsula campaign was over. Confederate losses were heavier than those sustained by the Union, but McClellan had fumbled away victory. He informed Washington during the campaign that he was outnumbered two to one, whereas the reverse was true. A little more energy on his part and the war might have ended or been drastically shortened.

The U.S. Navy at least could be proud of its role in the campaign. Not only had it safeguarded the supply line for the Army of the Potomac, but its gunboats had actively supported the troops ashore, at Malvern Hill, White Oak Swamp, and other locations.

On July 6, Capt. Charles Wilkes took command of an augmented group of gunboats on the James, now known as the James River Flotilla, to continue as a division of the North Atlantic Blockading Squadron under Flag Officer Goldsborough. Wilkes's flotilla continued to protect McClellan's troops on the peninsula, until the last were evacuated to northern Virginia in August.

The *Monitor*, after undergoing a refit, continued in service. On December 31 she was under tow by the *Rhode Island* off Cape Hatteras, North Carolina, on her way to Charleston when at 8:00 P.M. a violent storm broke. For three hours her crew struggled to save the ship, but the pumps were insufficient for the rush of water, and she went down in the gale that produced 30-foot waves. Most of her crew was rescued. The wreck has since been located and is a protected National Historic Site. In her relatively short period of service, the *Monitor* had wide influence. After the battle between the *Monitor* and the *Virginia*, the North succumbed to "monitor fever." Of eighty-four ironclads laid down by the North during the war, sixty-four were of the *Monitor* or turreted type.

Three weeks after the duel between the *Monitor* and *Virginia*, the navy contracted for ten improved Ericsson monitors. Both the *Passaic* and *Canonicus* classes were essentially modified monitors. The ten-ship *Passaic*-class monitors displaced 2,335 tons each and were 200' between perpendiculars 46' in beam and drew only 11' 6". They were designed to mount 2 x 15-inch Dahlgren guns, but several carried 1 x 11-inch or 1 x 8-inch Parrott rifled gun instead of the second 15-incher. They saw more service than any other Civil War monitors and were in both the North and South Atlantic Blockading Squadrons. They also participated in combined operations against Charleston and Savannah and in the Battle of Mobile Bay.

The USS *Passaic*. This highly successful ten-ship class mounted 1 x 15-inch and 1 x 11-inch Dahlgrens in their single turrets. *ORN*, series 1, vol. 8 (Washington, DC: Government Printing Office, 1899), 342.

The 9-ship *Canonicus* class, only 7 of which were commissioned, were 2,100-ton ships. Most were 235' x 43' 8" in size and mounted 2 x 15-inch Dahlgren smoothbores. Ericsson also designed the large single-turreted *Dictator* and *Puritan*. Commissioned in November 1864, the *Dictator* weighed 4,438 tons, was 312' x 50', and was armed with 2 x 15-inch Dahlgren smoothbores. She had 15 inches of armor on her turret, 12 inches on the pilothouse, 6 inches on the sides, and 1.5 inches on her deck. The *Puritan* was the largest of the Ericsson monitors; she weighed 4,912 tons, was 340' x 40' in size, and was designed to carry 2 x 20-inch smoothbore Dahlgren guns, which did not see service in the war.

Launched in July 1864, the *Puritan* was never commissioned and was officially rebuilt as a new ship in 1874.

Not all Union monitors were successful. The 20 *Casco*-class ironclads with turtleback decks, designed by Alban C. Stimers, were 1,175 tons and 225' x 45' 9". They floated with only 3 inches of freeboard before being fitted for turrets and had to have their decks sharply raised. Most were delivered after the war's end. Some later served without turrets and were armed with spar torpedoes; all were scrapped within about 10 years.

Among later Union ironclad designs were the *Keokuk* and *Dunderberg*. The *Keokuk*, designed by Ericsson's partner, C. W. Whitney, was a turtlebacked design. She mounted a 1 x 11-inch Dahlgren in each of two circular, turretlike, fixed armored gunhouses. But the weakness of her design lay in her armor: horizontal iron bars alternated with wood and the whole was covered with iron plate. She proved so vulnerable to heavy close-range fire that she sank after her first day in battle off Charleston.

The ironclad ram *Dunderberg*, a 7,060-ton warship, was a brigantine-rigged casemate ironclad designed for broadside fire. She had a double bottom, a collision bulkhead, and a massive solid-oak ram. Although laid down late in 1862, she was so delayed in construction that the navy rejected her in 1865. Her builder then sold her to France where, renamed the *Rochambeau*, she took part in the naval blockade of Prussia in 1870.

Monitors also appeared for western river use, and James Eads designed what were probably the most successful of Union monitors. Shortly after the *Monitor–Virginia* battle, Eads obtained a government contract to design and build three single-turreted monitors. The *Ozark* of 578 tons combined a single turret with 2 x 11-inch Dahlgrens and a casemate with 1 x 10-inch and 3 x 9-inch smoothbores. The other two, the 523-ton *Neosho* and *Osage*, were unique in being propelled by stern wheels, which, however, would not allow full 360-degree fire for the two turret-mounted 11-inch Dahlgrens.

Eads secured a contract to build four double-turreted river monitors. These *Milwaukee*-class monitors had one turret by Eads and the other by Ericsson. The forward-mounted Eads turret, of sophisticated design, turned on a ball-bearing race and used steam power for moving and elevating the guns and operating the gunport shutters and an elevator that dropped the guns to a lower deck for reloading. Laid down in 1862, they were commissioned in the spring of 1864. They had 8-inch turrets and 1.5-inch deck armor and were armed with 4 x 11-inch guns.

Perhaps the most unusual turret design of the war was on the Union warship *Roanoke*. Cut down from the wooden sloop of war of the same name, she was rebuilt with three centerline turrets. Unlike the original *Monitor*, she had high freeboard and thus was not a monitor-type vessel. Unstable and of deep draft, she was retained at New York City to protect that harbor against a possible Confederate attack.

The U.S. Navy would retain its coastal monitors into the twentieth century. Unfortunately, the Civil War monitor craze inhibited the construction of seagoing ironclads. Until the 1880s no seagoing vessels could fight ironclads. As noted, broadside ironclads were the exception in the Union navy; only one, the *New Ironsides*, was in the navy during the war, despite the fact

The USS *New Ironsides*, the most powerful warship of the Civil War. Naval Historical Center. NH 66759

that this type of vessel had a considerable tactical advantage in offensive power. The third of the Union experimental ironclads, she was not as much a break with tradition as the *Monitor*, but she was actually a far more successful ship type. She proved her worth in sixteen months of service with the South Atlantic Blockading Squadron off Charleston.

The *New Ironsides* was launched in May and commissioned in August 1862. Designed by Barnabas Bartol for Merrick & Sons of Philadelphia, she was much more conventional in appearance. An armored, broadside vessel, she was closely patterned after the French *Gloire*. With a beam of 56', the *New Ironsides* was 230' in length between perpendiculars, of which 170' was armored in a 4.5-inch iron belt. She had a draft of 15' 8" and displaced 3,500 tons. Boasting an iron ram on her prow, she had a formidable battery of 14 x 11-inch Dahlgren smoothbores and 2 x 150-pounder Parrott rifles. She was, in fact, the most powerful warship of the U.S. Navy in the Civil War. The *New Ironsides* was slow—only 7 knots instead of the design-specified 10 knots—but this was a consequence of her bulky hull, necessary to ensure shallow draft, a prerequisite for coastal operations.

The *New Ironsides* was far superior to the *Monitor* and her successors in seaworthiness, armament, and even in armor. The *Monitor* had laminated armor that Ericsson chose for speedy construction, but the *New Ironsides* utilized superior solid plate. The only advantages of the monitors were their more shallow draft and the fact that they presented such small targets.

Off Charleston, the "guardian of the blockade," as the *New Ironsides* came to be known, proved an effective deterrent to Confederate ironclad attacks against the wooden Union blockading fleet. Clearly her service there was unmatched by any other Union warship. Always the primary target for return fire during Union bombardments of Confederate shore positions, the *New Ironsides* came off with only minor damage, while the monitors often suffered severely and even, in some cases, fatally.

The *New Ironsides* could put at least ten times the firepower on target per hour as the *Monitor* and five times as much as the later *Passaic*-class monitors; this fire also could be concentrated. While the 15-inch guns of the *Passaic*-class monitors were much more powerful individually than the 11-inchers on the *New Ironsides*, the monitors would be at a severe disadvantage in trying to fight at sea. The earliest monitors had only 1 to 2 feet of freeboard, and even the "seagoing" monitors had only 2 feet and 7 inches The *New Ironsides* had 13 feet of freeboard, putting the bores of her guns 9 or 10 feet above water, where there was no fear of interference by the sea. Her higher freeboard also enabled the *New Ironsides* to keep her speed in a seaway. And, despite her unarmored ends, with her solid-plate armor she was the equal of any monitor defensively. She also did not have the weakness of possible turret jamming as on the monitors. Such advantages would have been critical had the Confederacy been able to acquire the "Laird rams" being built in Britain. Although smaller than the French *Gloire* or British *Warrior*, the *New Ironsides* was their equal in armor protection and superior to them in armament. The European ships had the advantage only in speed. The Confederates countered with casemated vessels along the lines of the *Virginia*, including the *Arkansas*, *Manassas*, *Atlanta*, *Nashville*, and *Tennessee*.

After the failure of McClellan's peninsula campaign, Lincoln ordered the general to bring his army back north in favor of a direct push south from Washington toward Richmond. Before the North could concentrate its forces, however, the Confederates defeated a Union army in the Second Battle of Manassas (Bull Run, August 29–30). Lee then invaded the North, but Union forces halted him and the Army of Northern Virginia at Sharpsburg (Antietam Creek, September 17).

The Union took the offensive again but was rebuffed at Fredericksburg (December 13) in Lee's most lopsided victory of the war. Lee won a brilliant victory against heavy odds at Chancellorsville (May 2–4, 1863) and then invaded the North for a second time in a spoiling attack, only to be stopped by the Army of the Potomac under Gen. George Meade at Gettysburg (July 1–3) in what turned out to be the high-water mark of the Confederacy.

NOTES

1. *Official Records of the Union and Confederate Navies in the War of the Rebellion* (hereinafter cited as *ORN*), series 2, vol. 2 (Washington, DC: Government Printing Office, 1921), 69.

2. Ivan Musicant, *Divided Waters: The Naval History of the Civil War* (New York: HarperCollins, 1995), 69.

3. Ibid.

4. Buchanan to Mallory, March 27, 1862, *ORN*, series 1, vol. 7 (Washington, DC: Government Printing Office, 1897), 44.

5. John Taylor Wood, "The First Fight of Iron-Clads," in *Battles and Leaders of the Civil War*, 4 vols., ed. Robert U. Johnson and Clarence C. Buel (Secaucus, NJ: Castle Books, 1956), 1:707.

6. Ibid., 702.

7. James Tertius deKay, *Monitor* (New York: Walker and Co., 1997), 193.

8. U.S. Navy Department, Naval History Division, *Civil War Naval Chronology, 1861–1865* (Washington, DC: Government Printing Office, 1971), 2:31.

9. Quoted in Wood, "The First Fight of Iron-Clads," 692.

Chapter Three

The Capture of New Orleans, April 1862

FIGHTING IN THE western theater had begun early. In contrast to the relatively limited cooperation between Union blue-water and land forces in the east, there was a major and effective collaboration between Union riverine naval forces and troops in the west to secure control of the great interior rivers, especially the Mississippi. But first, a river squadron of gunboats had to be constructed. Because of superior manufacturing resources, the Union built its ships first.

Paid for with army funds and technically under its command, the first of these were converted river steamers. Their conversion included reinforcing their decks so that they could carry heavy guns. Thick oak also was installed as protection against rifle fire; as a result, the vessels became known as "timberclads." But little could be done to protect their vulnerable boilers and engines. Then, in early August 1861, James Eads signed a contract to build seven gunboats. The first specific-built ironclads in the Western Hemisphere, all were completed in the fall.

Tennessee, with its important natural resources, food, and men, was vital to both sides. In January 1862, Union troops gained control of much of Kentucky, and the next month in a textbook operation, Union troops under Brig. Gen. Ulysses S. Grant and a gunboat flotilla under Commodore Andrew H. Foote moved against Confederate positions on the Tennessee and Cumberland Rivers. The subsequent Union successes owed much to the excellent relationship between these two Union commanders.

Utilizing the timberclads and new ironclads, Foote attacked and took Fort Henry on the Tennessee on February 6, 1862, although most of its garrison escaped to nearby Fort Donelson on the Cumberland River. The Union success at Henry was something of a fluke; the Confederates had been outgunned, and their principal battery had been badly sited close to the water.

However, Fort Donelson, the major defense of Nashville, was well sited on high ground, and its projectiles hit the sloping armor of the ironclads at right angles. Consequently, Foote's attack was repulsed. But, after four days of siege, on February 16, Donelson and his fourteen thousand-man garrison surrendered to the Union army. This defeat opened the way for Union forces to take Nashville, the first Confederate state capital in Union hands, as well as to secure access to middle Tennessee and some of the richest territory of the Confederacy.

These defeats necessitated withdrawal of Confederate forces from Columbus, Kentucky, which cleared the way for Union forces to move down the Mississippi River. In March a Union army under Gen. John Pope forced the Confederates to evacuate positions at New Madrid, and a water-land siege of nearby Island No. 10 began.

After taking Island No. 10, Foote's squadron pressed down the Mississippi and laid siege to Fort Pillow. There, on May 10, Capt. James Montgomery's eight ram gunboats staged a surprise attack on the Union squadron. Two Union ironclads were sunk in shallow water but were later refloated and soon repaired. Three Confederate warships were disabled by Union fire but got away downriver. Apart from far heavier personnel losses, the South had achieved a tactical victory. This Battle of Plum Point Bend was the war's first real engagement between naval squadrons. By the end of May the Confederates had abandoned Corinth, Mississippi, leaving Fort Pillow outflanked and untenable. On June 4 the Confederate defenders evacuated, taking what supplies and equipment they could and destroying the rest.

On June 5, Flag Officer Charles Davis, who had taken over from Foote, led his flotilla, reinforced by the seven ships of Col. Charles Ellet's Army Mississippi Ram Fleet, south to Memphis. The next day the Union squadron destroyed the Confederate defenders in perhaps the most lopsided naval engagement of the entire war. Memphis then surrendered, giving the North control of the fifth largest city in the Confederacy along with important manufacturing resources, including a former Confederate naval yard, which soon became a principal Union base. The Confederates were also forced to destroy the ironclad *Tennessee*, which they had been building there. However, they were able before the battle to remove downriver the second uncompleted ironclad, the *Arkansas*, to prevent its capture. Memphis also brought the Union control of key rail lines. The Mississippi was now open as far south as Vicksburg.

While Union naval forces were working their way south along the Mississippi, another squadron was taking the river's mouth in what undoubtedly was the most important Union naval victory in the western theater and one of the most important of the entire war. New Orleans was the Confederacy's most important seaport and its largest and wealthiest city. Beyond denying this outlet to the South, securing the entire Mississippi would split off the Trans-Mississippi West and open the river to goods from the northwest, binding that region firmly to the Union cause.

The chief advocates of an assault up the Mississippi River against New Orleans were U.S. Assistant Secretary of the Navy Gustavus Fox and Commander David D. Porter. They secured the approval of Secretary of the Navy Welles. The three met in conference with General McClellan and President Lincoln. McClellan was opposed, unless the army force proposed under Maj. Gen. Benjamin F. Butler only occupied New Orleans, defending there after the navy would have successfully run past the Confederate forts at the river's mouth. Lincoln agreed and that plan was approved. Secretary Welles called David G. Farragut to Washington and offered him command of the expedition. Farragut immediately accepted.

An outstanding officer and staunch Unionist, Farragut had spent fifty-one of his sixty years in the navy. Sponsored as a midshipman by his guardian, Commodore David Porter, he had served with Porter on the *Essex* during the War of 1812 and participated in the 1814 action in which she was defeated by HMS *Phoebe* and *Cherub*, one of the most sanguinary frigate actions in naval history. After that conflict he had seen varied service and had an exemplary record. A resident of Norfolk when Virginia seceded from the Union, Farragut had denounced the action and abandoned his home and possessions to travel north. Regardless, some in the navy doubted his commitment to the Union cause. Secretary Welles was not among them.

Farragut took up his new post at Ship Island, Mississippi, on February 20. When he appointed Farragut, Welles divided the Gulf Blockading Squadron into two separate commands, East and West. The previous commander, Flag Officer William McKean, who was ill and awaiting relief, retained the East Squadron. Operating from Key West, it would have responsibility for the Florida coast. Farragut's West Gulf Coast Blockading Squadron covered the remainder of the Gulf Coast all the way west to the Rio Grande.

Dividing the command meant that each man could concentrate on a smaller area, with more effective results. The division also enabled Welles to send Farragut to the Gulf without telegraphing his plan of taking New Orleans. This cover was only partly successful, however, for an aggressive commander such as Farragut was unlikely to remain idle for long.

An energetic, "hands-on," and capable commander who liked to be seen with his men and instruct them, Farragut was a careful planner and a bold leader. He spent nearly a month preparing for the expedition. Flying his flag in the screw sloop *Hartford*, Farragut, for the attempt against New Orleans, would command 17 ships mounting 193 guns. The most powerful of these were 8 steam sloops and corvettes: *Brooklyn* (26 guns), *Hartford* (28), *Iroquois* (11), *Mississippi* (22), *Oneida* (10), *Pensacola* (25), *Richmond* (22), and *Varuna* (11). These mounted in all 155 guns. There also were 9 gunboats: *Cayuga* (4), *Itasca* (4), *Katahdin* (4), *Kennebec* (4), *Kineo* (4), *Pinola* (5), *Sciota* (5), *Winona* (4), and *Wissahickon* (4). Farragut also had a squadron of 20 mortar schooners under Commander Porter, his foster brother. Maj. Gen. Benjamin Butler's 10,000 troops accompanied the expedition.

On April 16, following careful planning and preparations, Farragut moved his ships from the Gulf into the Mississippi River estuary, just below and out of range of the river forts. Farragut planned that, once the forts had been passed, Butler's troops would join the squadron through a bayou about five miles above the forts. Thus, Union warships and troops would be between the forts and New Orleans. But for the ships to pass the forts, there would have to be a close-range engagement.

Confederate leaders in Richmond, including Mallory, would have considerable responsibility for the loss of the Crescent City. They believed that the principal threat on the river was from the north and so sent their scant resources there. This miscalculation also contributed to the Confederate failure to complete the ironclads *Louisiana* and *Mississippi*.

The U.S. Navy side-wheel frigate *Mississippi*. Commissioned in 1841, she participated in Farragut's operation up the Mississippi River. Wash drawing by Clary Ray showing the ship during the Civil War. Naval Historical Center. NH 60655

The key to the defense of New Orleans, guarding the southern Mississippi, was Forts Jackson and St. Philip, manned by a total of some eleven hundred men. Jackson, a star-shaped stone and mortar fortification, was situated some one hundred yards from the levee on the right or west bank of the river. It mounted seventy-four guns. Fort St. Philip, a brick and stone work covered with sod, stood on the opposite bank about one-half mile upstream and mounted fifty-two guns. High water in the river, however, had flooded parts of both forts. Confederate engineers did what they could, working around the clock to control the water and strengthen the forts against an expected Union attack. Brig. Gen. Johnson K. Duncan commanded the land defenses. His forts were manned by inexperienced and largely untrained soldiers, which would have its effects in the battle to come, especially in conditions of poor visibility.

On the river itself the Confederates mustered fourteen vessels, but most were very small and they mounted a total of only

forty guns. Capt. John A. Stephenson commanded the Confederate River Defense Fleet, which consisted of six small, makeshift
gunboats, converted river tugs with iron-reinforced prows for
ramming: *Defence*, *General Breckinridge*, *General Lovell*, *Resolute*,
Stonewall Jackson, and *Warrior*. They mounted only seven guns
total. The Louisiana State Navy provided the side-wheel steamer
gunboats *Governor Moore* and *General Quitman*, mounting two
guns each.

The Confederate navy added six vessels under river commander Flag Officer John K. Mitchell. Two of these were ironclads,
only one of which was in place when the Union attack began.
She was the thinly armored (1.5 inches) ironclad ram *Manassas*
with one gun. Then, on April 22, after the Union assault of the river
had commenced, Mitchell arrived with the ironclad *Louisiana*.

The *Louisiana* was the only real threat to the Union squadron.
Many in New Orleans regarded her, after the forts, as the strongest defense for the city. Mallory had wanted to send her upriver,
but the question was moot; the *Louisiana* was unfinished at the
time of the Union attack, her four large steam engines yet to turn
over.

With a 45-degree-angle casemate, the *Louisiana* was an immense vessel at 264' x 62' and covered by 4-inch iron plate. Her
builder, C. C. Murray, planned a unique propulsion system of
two paddle wheels set in a well on the centerline, one abaft the
other, and two propellers. She also had twin rudders. Towed
downriver with mechanics still working on her, she was moored
to the shore north of Fort St. Philip when Union naval forces began their assault. Pierced for twenty-two guns, during the battle
she mounted sixteen: 2 x 7-inch rifles, 3 x 9-inch smoothbores, 4 x
8-inchers, and 7 x 32-pounder rifles. These were worked not by
sailors but by soldiers from the Crescent Artillery.

In addition to the two ironclads, Mitchell had two gunboats
mounting a total of ten guns, the *Jackson* (2 guns) and *McRae* (8),
and launches *No. 3* and *No. 6*, each with one gun. Stephenson
also had fire rafts ready to set loose on the current against the
Union fleet. The Confederates completed their defense by spread-
ing a great chain, supported by seven anchored hulks, across the
river. It ran from a point abreast of Fort Jackson to the opposite
shore.

A 13-inch mortar aboard a U.S. Navy mortar schooner, possibly in the operation against New Orleans. Library of Congress. B8184-10067

On the evening of April 18, Porter's 20 mortar boats, towed into position by 7 steamers and moored along the riverbank, began a bombardment of Fort Jackson. Each mounted a 13-inch mortar. These were formidable weapons. Each weighed 17,250 pounds and rested in a 4,500-pound bed. With a 20-pound charge of powder and at an elevation of 41 degrees, the mortar could hurl a 204-pound shell loaded with 7 pounds of powder 3 miles. At this range the shell took 30 seconds in flight. The mortars had been used earlier against Island No. 10 and Fort Pillow, but without notable success. Porter was convinced, however, they could reduce Forts St. Philip and Jackson. Such mortars also were used against Fort Pulaski, Georgia.

Anchored some 3,000 yards from Fort Jackson, the mortar boats were protected by a bend of the river and woods. Each vessel fired at the rate of 1 shell every 10 minutes. At night, to provide some rest, they fired 1 shell every half-hour. For 6 days and nights the great mortars hurled 16,800 shells, almost all of them at the fort and without much physical effect. At night the Confederates would send fire rafts down the river, but these were towed off by Union boats and did no damage.

Although Confederate guns on barbette mounts in the fort were disabled at one time or another by the Union shelling, for the most part the gunners heroically kept to their positions and remounted the guns. Indeed, effective counterbattery Confederate fire on the 19th sank the Union mortar schooner *Maria J. Carlton* and killed and wounded several Union sailors. Although not everyone shares his opinion, Porter believed that the first day's fire "was the most effective of any during the bombardment, and had the fleet been ready to move at once, the passage could have been effected without serious difficulty."[1] Although the Union bombardment accomplished little in a material sense, it did affect the Confederate gunners, exhausting them physically and emotionally.

The Union delay in running the gauntlet to New Orleans during this shelling caused considerable anxiety among sailors of the squadron, especially those who had never before experienced combat. Farragut's clerk, Bradley Osbon, had once commanded a ship in the Argentine Navy. After Farragut had returned from visiting one ship where morale seamed lagging, he ordered Osbon to that vessel, saying: "I hear they are as blue as indigo in that wardroom over there. . . . Tell them some stories of the fights you've been in and come out of alive. It will stir their blood and do them good."[2]

Too long a delay was not a good idea, however. Farragut grew impatient, and on the night of the 20th, he sent the screw gunboats *Itasca* and *Pinola* against the Confederate river obstructions. Under heavy but inaccurate Confederate fire, the crews on the two vessels managed to open a gap. Lt. Pierce Crosby of the *Pinola* attempted to blow up one of the hulks with a mine exploded by an electric wire, but the wire broke when the gunboat backed off. Lt. Charles Caldwell then brought the *Itasca* alongside another hulk, and some of the crew managed to break the chain with a chisel. Farragut believed that the resulting break would be sufficient for the fleet to pass through.

Meanwhile, the Union crews prepared their ships. Extra spars, rigging, boats, and all but a few sails were landed. Heavy iron cable chains were arranged on the outside of the vessels to provide additional protection to the engines and boilers, like chain mail armor. Bags of ashes, clothing, sand, or anything else readily available were packed around the vulnerable boilers. Were these to be punctured, a torrent of hot steam and personnel casualties would result and, important to the squadron as a whole, immobilize the vessel, perhaps jeopardizing the entire operation.

Weight was distributed aboard the ships so that they would draw less water aft than forward. This meant that if a vessel grounded while heading upstream, the bow would strike bottom first and the ship would not be turned around by the swift current. The crews also whitewashed the ships' decks so that the gunners' tools would stand out more clearly at night; at the same time, the hulls received coatings of oil and mud to render them more difficult to distinguish from the shore.

On April 20, Farragut issued a general order that called for the ships to run through the obstructions one at a time while Porter's mortar boats provided covering fire. The ships would then be between the forts and New Orleans. Once the ships were in position to protect the troops, forces would be landed at Quarantine from the Gulf side by bringing them through the bayou. Land and naval forces would move in tandem to New Orleans. Farragut reserved the option of reducing the forts if possible, but he told his captains that, unless otherwise ordered, they were to steam past them.

Farragut met with Porter on the 22nd and stated his intention to make the attempt that night. Porter pleaded for one additional day of shelling, and it was granted. But with the majority of the shells falling outside Fort Jackson, Farragut decided not to delay further. The attempt would be made on the 24th.

Osbon recalled the tension in the squadron the night of the 23rd: "At the usual hour the crews turned in, but I think there was little sleep. The men were cheerful and determined, but wakeful. Most of them had been green hands when we started, and scarcely one of them had been under fire. With a night attack just ahead it was natural that they should be anxious."[3]

Soon after midnight on the 24th, the crews on the ships were awakened and, at 1:55 A.M. aboard the *Hartford*, Farragut ordered Osbon to hoist two red lanterns as the signal for the squadron to get under way. The ships moved upriver in three divisions to pass through the obstructions in the opening made by the *Pinola* and *Itasca*. The first division, under Capt. Theodorus Bailey, consisted

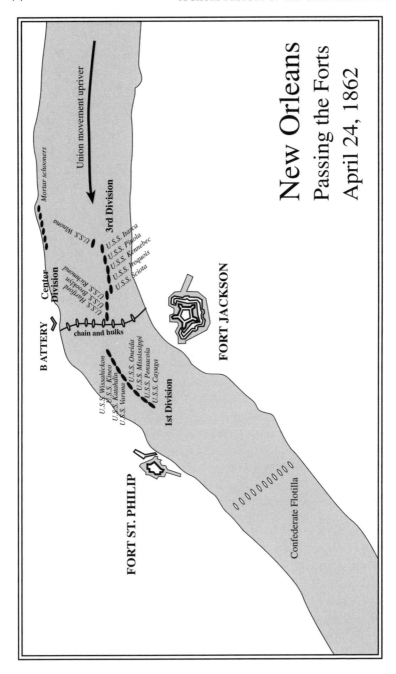

New Orleans
Passing the Forts
April 24, 1862

Union movement upriver

Mortar schooners

3rd Division

U.S.S. Winona
U.S.S. Itasca
U.S.S. Pinola
U.S.S. Kennebec
U.S.S. Iroquois
U.S.S. Sciota

Center
Division

U.S.S. Hartford
U.S.S. Brooklyn
U.S.S. Richmond

BATTERY

chain and hulks

FORT JACKSON

U.S.S. Wissahickon
U.S.S. Kineo
U.S.S. Katahdin
U.S.S. Varuna
U.S.S. Oneida
U.S.S. Mississippi
U.S.S. Pensacola
U.S.S. Cayuga

1st Division

FORT ST. PHILIP

Confederate Flotilla

of the *Cayuga* (his flagship), *Pensacola, Mississippi, Oneida, Varuna, Katahdin, Kineo,* and *Wissahickon.* The second division, under Farragut, was composed of the *Hartford, Brooklyn,* and *Richmond.* The third division, under Capt. Henry H. Bell, included the *Sciota, Iroquois, Kennebec, Pinola, Itasca,* and *Winona.* The *Cayuga* was the first ship through the Confederate hulks, at about 3:30. She was not discovered until about ten minutes later, when she was well under both forts. General Duncan at Fort Jackson subsequently complained that Mitchell had not sent any fire rafts down to light the river at night, nor had he stationed any vessel below the forts to warn of the Union fleet's approach. Certainly, the three different Confederate naval commands and the lack of cooperation between land and naval commanders proved costly.

As soon as they spotted the *Cayuga,* the Confederate gunners opened up with all their guns, and the Union ships replied. Soon the water was covered in thick smoke from the black powder charges, which obscured vision on both sides. But Porter had brought forward five mortar steamers that opened fire some two hundred yards from Fort Jackson, pouring into it grape, canister, and shrapnel shell, "while the mortars threw in their bombs with great fury."[4] This assault drove many Confederates from their guns and reduced the effectiveness of the gun crews who remained.

The second ship through, the *Pensacola,* had been slow to get under way, leaving the *Cayuga* to face the full fury of the Confederate fire alone. The pilot of the *Cayuga,* Lt. George H. Perkins, had the presence of mind to note that the Confederate guns had been laid so that their fire was concentrated on the middle of the river. He steered his vessel closer to the walls of Fort St. Philip, and although the masts and rigging of his ship were shot up, the hull was little damaged.

The *Pensacola*'s captain, Henry W. Morris, apparently interpreted Farragut's orders as meaning that he was to engage the forts. He halted the ship in the middle of the obstructions and let loose a broadside against Fort St. Philip, driving Confederate gunners to safety. On clearing the obstructions, he ordered a second broadside against the fort. But when she stopped dead in the water, the *Pensacola* became a perfect target. She took nine shots in her hull, and her rigging and masts were much cut up.

She also suffered four men killed and thirty-three wounded, more than on any other Union ship in the operation. Executive Officer Lt. Francis Asbury Roe recalled, "The guns' crews, right under me, were decimated. The groans, shrieks, and wails of the dying and wounded were so horrible that I shudder now at the recollection of it."[5] The remaining Union ships followed, their guns blazing and firing grape and canister as well as round shot. The Confederate batteries had difficulty finding the range, and damage and casualties aboard these vessels were slight.

"Splendid Naval Triumph on the Mississippi." U.S. Navy ships running past Forts St. Philip and Jackson on their way to New Orleans, April 24, 1862. Lithograph by Currier & Ives, 1862. Naval Historical Center. NH 76369-KN

At about 4:00 A.M. the Confederate vessels in the Mississippi joined the fray. The *McRae* was anchored along the shore some three hundred yards above Fort St. Philip when lookouts spotted the *Cayuga* moving through the obstructions. The *McRae's* captain, Lt. Thomas B. Huger, ordered her cables slipped and opened fire. The *McRae's* largest gun was a 9-inch Dahlgren on a pivot mount. She also had six 32-pounders in broadsides and a 6-pounder rifled gun. The *McRae* opened up with her port battery and pivot gun, but the latter burst on its tenth round. The *Cayuga* passed by her, and then two other Union ships appeared, probably the *Varuna* and *Oneida*. They steamed past without opening fire, probably taking the *McRae* for a Union gunboat. The Confederate gunboat sheered to port, then starboard, delivering two broadsides. Both the *Varuna* and *Oneida* sheered to starboard and returned fire. Each mounted two 11-inch Dahlgrens in pivot, and these soon made the difference. One of their shells started a fire in the *McRae*'s sail room. Only desperate efforts kept the blaze from reaching the magazine.

Most of the Confederate warships fled north on the approach of the Union squadron. Their captains believed they had little choice with their small, lightly armed vessels. Lt. Alexander Warley, captain of the ironclad *Manassas*, was determined to attack, even if it was alone. Among Confederate naval officers on the river, he alone understood that the best course of action was an immediate combined attack by gunboats and fire rafts to immobilize the Union vessels long enough for the heavy guns in the two forts to destroy them. The *Manassas* was moored to the left bank of the river above Fort St. Philip, when gun flashes in the vicinity of the chain at about 3:00 A.M. indicated action in progress. Warley ordered the *Manassas* to get under way and stand downriver.

Warley was determined to halt Farragut's squadron so that the forts could engage it. His first attempt to ram had to be aborted when the Confederate *Resolute* steamed into her path. Warley then made a second attempt. Captain Morris of the *Pensacola* was startled to see the *Manassas* bearing down on his ship, but skillful maneuvering by the pilot just avoided a collision, and the *Pensacola* let loose with broadsides from her 9-inch Dahlgrens as she passed by. Although damaged in the exchange, the *Manassas* kept her station in the river.

Warley spotted another target, the side-wheeler *Mississippi*. Lt. George Dewey turned his ship toward the onrushing Confederate ram, confident "that our superior tonnage must sink her if we struck her fairly."[6] The ram was more agile than the paddler, however, and avoided the Union parry while striking the *Mississippi* a glancing blow on her port side. When the Union ship righted, Dewey could see a large hole in his ship and immediately yelled to his crew to man the pumps, but the *Mississippi* was not leaking. Dewey recalled that "the impact of the ram, which would have sunk any other ship in the fleet, had taken out a section of solid timber seven feet long, four feet broad, and four inches deep. About fifty copper bolts had been cut as clean as if they were hair under a razor's edge. I remember seeing their bright, gleaming ends when I looked down from the hurricane deck in my first glimpse of that hole in our side."[7]

Heavy fire from the forts was answered by broadsides from the flotilla. As the Union ships cleared the forts, they next came under fire from the Confederate ironclad *Louisiana* moored along the riverbank. Her gunports were constructed so that she did not have a wide arc of fire and thus scored few hits. The *Cayuga* then swept north, overtaking some of the fleeing Confederate squadron and firing into them. Three of the Confederate gunboats struck and ran ashore. The *Varuna* and *Oneida* now arrived and, in the confusion, the *Varuna* mistook the *Cayuga* for a Confederate vessel and fired a broadside on her.

Impatient with the slow progress of the *Pensacola*, meanwhile, Farragut ordered the *Hartford* past her, and he climbed into the mizzen rigging to have a better view over the smoke. Osbon recalled the scene:

> Shot, shell, grape, and canister filled the air with deadly missiles. It was like the breaking up of the universe, with the moon and all the stars bursting in our midst. As for seeing what the other vessels were doing, or what was going on about us, that was impossible. In that blinding smoke, and night, with everything flying in all directions, the only thing we could see was the flash of guns in our faces and the havoc on our own ship. Ropes were swinging, splinters were flying. . . . At first the enemy's aim had been high, but now they lowered it until their fire began to cut us through.[8]

As the *Hartford* moved north, Farragut saw a blazing fire raft bearing down on the port bow, pushed by the unarmed Confederate tug *Moser*. Farragut cried out for the *Hartford* to turn to starboard, but she was too close to the shore and her bow immediately grounded hard on a mud bank. Capt. Horace Sherman of the *Moser*, using his advantage, positioned the fire raft against the *Hartford*'s port side. This maneuver soon ignited the paint on the ship's side, which blazed up and caught the rigging. With his ship on fire and immobilized, Farragut thought that the *Hartford* was doomed. Fortunately for him, the gunners at Fort St. Philip were unable to fire into the now stationary target because the fleet's fire had dismounted one of its largest guns and another could not be brought to bear.

View on gun deck of U.S. Navy screw sloop *Hartford*, 1864, showing her 9-inch Dahlgren broadside guns. Naval Historical Center. NH 53678

Farragut now came down from the rigging and went up and down the decks encouraging his men to fight the fire. Shells from the *Hartford*'s guns, meanwhile, soon sent the *Moser* to the bottom. As Capt. Richard Wainwright directed fire-fighting efforts, Bradley Osbon brought up three shells, unscrewed their fuses, and dropped them over the gunwale of the *Hartford* into the fire raft. Their explosions tore holes in the raft, sinking her and, in the process, extinguishing the flames. The fires on the *Hartford* were also put out, and she backed off the mud bank. Her crew cheered wildly and took to the guns as the sloop resumed her course upriver, away from the forts.

In the confusion and smoke, two accidents occurred. The gunboat *Kineo* collided with the sloop *Brooklyn*; but, despite serious damage, the *Kineo* was able to continue past the gauntlet of the forts. The *Brooklyn*, meanwhile, plowed into one of the hulks. She suddenly ground to a halt north of the obstructions. Her anchor had caught in the hulk and the hawser went taut. The current caught the sloop, turning her broadside to Fort St. Philip. She had been hit several times, and gunners in the fort appeared to have her range when a crewman on the sloop managed to cut the cable, freeing her.

Capt. Thomas T. Craven of the *Brooklyn* took his ship close to Fort St. Philip, firing three broadsides into the Confederate works as the sloop passed. Further upstream, the *Brooklyn* almost grazed the *Louisiana* as she went by her, the two ships exchanging fire at very close quarters. A 9-inch shell from the *Louisiana* struck the *Brooklyn* just above the waterline, but it failed to explode. Later, the *Brooklyn*'s crew discovered that the Confederate gunners had failed to remove a lead patch from the fuse.

The smoke from the firing was now so thick that it was virtually impossible to take any bearings. Craven merely turned his ship toward the noise and flashes of light ahead. But the tide took the sloop over on the lee shore and in perfect position for the guns of Fort Jackson. As the sloop touched bottom, Craven could see the *Manassas* emerging from the smoke toward his own ship.

Warley previously had tried to ram the *Hartford* but without success. The *Manassas* had taken a number of shell hits, and her smokestack was riddled, sharply reducing her speed and making it virtually impossible for her to prevent any more Union ships from passing upriver. Warley resolved to take his vessel downriver and attack Porter's now unprotected mortar boats. But when the Confederate forts mistakenly fired on the ironclad, Warley thought better of the idea and decided to return upriver. It was at that point that he had spotted the *Brooklyn* lying athwart the river and headed for Fort Jackson. He ordered resin thrown into the furnaces to get up as much speed as possible and maneuvered his ship to pin the *Brooklyn* against the riverbank.

When seamen aboard the *Brooklyn* spotted the approaching ram and gave the alarm, Craven ordered the sloop's helm turned, but he could only lessen, not avoid, impact. Only moments before the collision, a shot from a 32-pounder carronade aboard the *Manassas* crashed into the *Brooklyn* but was stopped by sandbags piled around the steam drum.

The *Manassas* caught the *Brooklyn* at a slight angle, crushing three planks and driving the chain that had been strung into the ship's side. The blow was such that Craven was certain his ship would go down, but the chain and a full coal bunker helped lessen the impact. Meanwhile, the *Manassas* was able to disengage and resume her progress upriver.

The tail of Farragut's force, Porter's mortar flotilla, was also under way. This division included the sailing sloop *Portsmouth*, which was towed by tugs. Coming under fire as they approached Fort Jackson, Porter ordered the mortar boats stopped and opened fire at about 4:20 A.M. The mortars fired for about one-half hour, sufficient time, it was thought, for the squadron to have cleared the forts. When Porter signaled for the mortars to stop firing, however, some of the Union ships were still engaging the forts.

Thick smoke obscured vision, and the *Wissahickon*, the last vessel in the first division, grounded. As the sun rose, her captain, Lt. Albert N. Smith, discovered his ship near three third-division ships, the *Iroquois*, *Sciota*, and *Pinola*, but also near the Confederate gunboat *McRae*. The gunboat was soon hotly engaged with the much more heavily gunned *Iroquois* and paid the price. His ship was badly damaged and Lieutenant Huger, captain of the *McRae*, was mortally wounded; three other men were killed outright and seventeen were wounded.

At this point the *Manassas* came on the scene. Warley had tried to ram the *Iroquois*, but the Union ship easily avoided her. Warley persisted, however, maneuvering to ram the other Union ships. All the Union captains, realizing their danger if they were to be disabled close to the Confederate forts, abandoned their efforts against the *McRae* and resumed their passage upriver.

Three of Farragut's ships failed to make it past the forts. The *Kennebec* and *Itasca* ran afoul of the river obstructions. When the *Itasca* tried to back clear, she collided with the *Winona*. The *Itasca* also took a 42-pounder shot through her boiler and had to abandon the effort. The *Winona* was able to retire under cover of darkness; the *Kennebec*, caught between the two Confederate forts at daybreak, also withdrew. Fourteen of the ships in Farragut's squadron of seventeen vessels had made it past the forts, however.

Farragut lost one other ship, the screw steamer *Varuna*. At about 4:00, Lt. Beverly Kennon of the Louisiana State gunboat *Governor Moore* spotted the *Varuna* of the first division. Faster than a number of the Union ships, she was out ahead by herself. Kennon immediately moved to attack her, but to reach the *Varuna*, the *Governor Moore* was forced to run a hail of shot and shell from other Union ships, which cut her up badly and killed and wounded a number of her crew. The exchange of fire also produced so much smoke that the Confederate gunboat was able to escape and follow the *Varuna* upriver.

The two opposing vessels then found themselves almost alone on the river. They were some six hundred yards ahead of the trailing Union ships. The *Governor Moore* was behind the *Varuna* by some one hundred yards. The Union warship engaged her adversary with her sternchaser and repeatedly tried to sheer to get off a broadside. But by closely following the motions of her enemy, the *Governor Moore* was able to mirror the movements and avoid being hit.

Nonetheless, the *Governor Moore* took a terrific pounding from the *Varuna*'s sternchaser, shots from which killed or wounded two-thirds of those on the forecastle. With his own ship only forty yards from his adversary and his bow 32-pounder unable to bear because of the close range, Kennon ordered the muzzle depressed to fire a shell at the Union warship through his own ship's deck. This shot had a devastating effect, raking the *Varuna*.

Kennon then ordered a second shell fired, with similar result. With the two ships only about ten feet apart, after loosing a round from her aft pivot gun, the *Varuna* sheered off to starboard to loose a broadside, but Kennon, on top of the hurricane deck, could see her mastheads above the smoke and knew what was intended. He swung his own ship hard to port and smashed into the Union vessel. Kennon recalled, "The crushing noise made by her breaking ribs told how amply we were repaid for all we had lost and suffered."[9]

The *Governor Moore* then backed off and rammed the *Varuna* again, this time taking a full broadside from the Union ship and making most of the men on the weather deck casualties. Shortly thereafter, however, another Confederate warship, the River Defense Fleet gunboat *Stonewall Jackson* appeared, ramming the

Varuna on her opposite (port) side. This third blow produced such damage that the pumps were unable to keep her afloat, and the *Varuna* was run ashore. For her pains, the *Stonewall Jackson* took two broadsides from the mortally wounded Union vessel and was herself soon sinking. Her captain ordered her run ashore and burned to prevent capture.

As he watched the *Varuna* ground, Kennon was faced with rapidly closing Union ships. Her adversaries soon subjected the *Governor Moore* to devastating fire. With his own ship in danger of going down in the river, Kennon made for the shore himself, grounding his vessel just above the stricken *Varuna*. He then ordered the *Governor Moore* burned. The casualty toll on the Confederate vessel was appalling: fifty-seven dead and seven wounded from a crew of ninety-three.

Dawn was breaking as the Union squadron assembled at Quarantine Station between 5:30 and 6:00 A.M. The *Manassas* was then sighted, making for the squadron. Standing on the hurricane deck of the *Mississippi*, Lieutenant Dewey saw the *Hartford*, blackened from fire, steaming by: "Farragut was in her rigging, his face eager with victory in the morning light and his eyes snapping. 'Run down the ram!' he called. I shall never forget that glimpse of him. He was a very urbane man. But it was plain that if we did not run the *Manassas* down, and promptly, he would not think well of us."[10] But when Warley saw all of Farragut's ships assembled, he knew that the fight was over. His own vessel's speed was much reduced, and she had sustained such damage that an attack would have been suicidal. As Warley remarked later: "My people had stood gallantly by me, and I owed to them a duty as well as to the country. I cut the delivery pipes, and headed the vessel inshore. . . . I had the opportunity of throwing my men into the swamp and getting them under the cover of the rise in the bank before the enemy commenced to grape [fire grapeshot] us, which they did for an hour and a half."[11]

The battle for the mouth of the Mississippi was over. With the Union fleet past the forts and the Confederate gunboats destroyed, no real barrier remained between Farragut's squadron and New Orleans. Union casualties were surprisingly light: the total from April 18 to 26 was only 39 killed and 171 wounded. After burying his dead and effecting minor repairs to his vessels, at 11:00 A.M. Farragut sent word to Butler to land his troops, leaving behind the gunboats *Kineo* and *Wissahickon* at Quarantine Station for support. He then ordered the squadron to get under way.

After a brief engagement with two shore batteries four miles below New Orleans, Farragut's squadron arrived at the Crescent City just after noon on April 25 and anchored. Confederate troops already had evacuated the city. With the river up and near the top of the levee, the Union guns could easily be brought to bear on New Orleans and the narrow neck that served as the land approach to the city. In any case, the city had no major food stocks. Faced with the inevitable, the city fathers announced they would not resist, and they surrendered New Orleans to the Union forces. Capt. Theodorus Bailey, accompanied only by Lt. George H. Perkins, went ashore through an angry mob to take surrender of the thoroughly disorganized city and hoist the U.S. flag. That same day the Confederates burned their unfinished ironclad, the *Mississippi*. Launched only on April 19 and fitted with 3.75-inch iron plate, she was to carry twenty guns, including 2 x 7-inch rifles, but her ordnance was never mounted.

Union troops had cut off Fort Jackson, and, on the 25th, Porter sent in an officer under flag of truce and demanded that General Duncan surrender the fort and the naval vessels in the vicinity, including the *Louisiana*. Duncan refused, so Porter commenced a heavy mortar bombardment. Early on the 28th the garrison mutinied and many men deserted. Later that day, Duncan surrendered both Fort Jackson and Fort St. Philip to Porter, whereupon Mitchell burned the *Louisiana* to prevent her capture, much to the disappointment of Farragut, who had hoped to use her against her former owners. The Confederate army officers assured Porter that the ironclad was not under their command and, hence, not bound by his surrender order.

Planning, leadership, and bold execution had given Farragut a great victory, and he became an immediate hero in the North. However, his success resulted from the sure knowledge that, once he had run past the Confederate forts, Union troops would be able to land and cut the defenders off from New Orleans.

The loss of its largest and most important seaport was a heavy blow to the Confederacy. The mighty river was now free from its mouth upriver to New Orleans for Union shipping. Vicksburg and Port Hudson were the only remaining Mississippi River Confederate strongholds.

On May 1, the same day that Butler's troops were landed in New Orleans, Farragut directed Porter to return to Ship Island with his mortar boat flotilla to prepare for movement to the Alabama coast for operations against Mobile Bay as soon as the big ships of the squadron could join him. Farragut also sent Captain Craven upriver in the *Brooklyn*, along with several gunboats. He instructed Craven to steam to Vicksburg and shell and destroy its large railroad center. The *Brooklyn* got past Baton Rouge without incident but, short of her destination, accompanying gunboats *Itasca* and *Sciota* developed engine problems, and, with his own ship having scraped the bottom of the river in several places, Craven turned back. Nearing Baton Rouge, the *Brooklyn* encountered the *Oneida*, under Commander S. Philip Lee, and two other gunboats, the *Pinola* and *Kennebec*. Lee had new orders from Farragut, who had learned that the river was dropping. He ordered Craven not to risk his ship and to go no further upriver than Baton Rouge. Soon afterward the *Iroquois*, under Commander James S. Palmer, also arrived, with additional orders. Farragut ordered Palmer to take Baton Rouge while Lee was to continue north and take Natchez, Mississippi. Craven was to wait just north of Baton Rouge until Farragut could arrive with additional warships.

Palmer sent ashore a landing party from the *Iroquois* and on May 8 seized the arsenal and took possession of Baton Rouge without a shot being fired. Farragut followed, lifting fifteen hundred infantry from New Orleans to secure the town. On the 13th the *Iroquois* and the *Oneida* took Natchez, as Farragut's squadron continued its progression toward Vicksburg, arriving near that place four days later. On the 18th, strengthened by reinforcements from troops evacuated from New Orleans and other points in Mississippi, Confederate authorities at Vicksburg rebuffed a demand for its surrender, beginning a yearlong Union water and land effort to take the stronghold. Farragut and most of the Union squadron then returned downriver.

Washington ordered Farragut to make another attempt to open the river, and he retraced his steps to Vicksburg, taking along mortar boats. On June 28 he ran a three-mile gauntlet of Confederate fire from the high bluffs on the east bank of the river at Vicksburg, sustaining considerable damage to his ships but linking up with Flag Officer Davis's Mississippi River Flotilla in the river above the city on July 1.

On July 15 the powerful Confederate ram *Arkansas*, removed from Memphis to prevent her capture in May and taken to Yazoo City for completion, sortied from the Yazoo River. Hastily constructed with poor engines, the *Arkansas* was 165' (between perpendiculars) x 35' x 11' 6". A casemated ironclad, she had a ram bow, but unlike the other Confederate ironclads, her casemate was perpendicular rather than sloped. She mounted eight guns: 2 x 9-inch Dahlgrens, 2 x 8-inch 64-pounders, 2 x 6-inch rifles, and 2 x 32-pounder smoothbores.

The CSS ram *Arkansas* running through the U.S. Navy squadron above Vicksburg, July 15, 1862, from *Battles and Leaders of the Civil War.* Naval Historical Center. NH 73378

Perhaps even to the surprise of her crew, the *Arkansas* proceeded to smash her way south through the entire Union fleet to Vicksburg. Farragut again ran past the forts at Vicksburg on the night of July 21–22 in an unsuccessful attempt to destroy the *Arkansas*. The ram took considerable damage in an exchange of fire with the *Essex* on the 22nd and from being rammed twice by the *Queen of the West*. Both Union ships, however, also were damaged in the exchange, especially by fire from shore batteries.

With the failure to destroy the *Arkansas*, Farragut gave up. Two days after the abortive attack on the Confederate ironclad, he embarked Union troops on transports and the entire fleet headed downriver. Farragut returned to New Orleans but left two gunboats, along with the *Essex* and the *Sumter*, at Baton Rouge in case the *Arkansas* ventured south.

Although damage from the July 22 attack was still being repaired and her engines were in terrible shape, on August 3 the *Arkansas* got underway for Baton Rouge with her executive officer, Lt. Henry K. Stevens, in command. The ironclad had been ordered to support an attack by three thousand Confederate troops under Maj. Gen. John C. Breckenridge. About the same number of Union troops, under Brig. Gen. Thomas Williams, manned entrenchments at Baton Rouge while four Union vessels, including the *Essex*, protected the city from the river side.

A day after the *Arkansas* started out, her engines broke down. As the ironclad anchored for repairs, Breckenridge's troops were breaching the Union lines and driving the Federal troops back against the river. The *Arkansas* finally got under way only to suffer another engine breakdown within sight of Baton Rouge. As her crew desperately tried to repair the engine, Union gunboats kept up a steady stream of fire against the advancing Confederate troops and forced them back, although Williams was killed.

During the night of the 5th, Capt. William Porter of the *Essex* learned of the presence of the *Arkansas*, and at 8:00 A.M. on the 6th he led the small Union squadron upriver against her. Her crew completed repairs to the *Arkansas* just as the *Essex* was getting up steam. But as the *Arkansas* moved to engage the *Essex*, her engines broke down yet again, and she drifted back to the shore. Stevens ordered his men to abandon ship after first firing the vessel. The *Arkansas* drifted into the river and downstream for more than an hour until she blew up. On learning of her destruction, Breckenridge decided not to renew the land attack and withdrew.

Attempts to take Vicksburg continued. At the end of 1862 and early in 1863, General Grant made several efforts with his Army of the Tennessee for amphibious operations. These efforts failed, but Grant moved down the Mississippi past Vicksburg, marched inland, and destroyed the major rail hub of Jackson. He then drove on Vicksburg from the east. The city finally fell to Union siege operations on July 4, along with over thirty thousand troops. With Vicksburg lost and his own remaining Mississippi stronghold surrounded by fourteen thousand Union troops, the commander of Port Hudson surrendered on July 9. The entire Mississippi was now under Union control, and the Confederacy was split.

Control of the mighty river greatly benefited the Union. Supplies from the Trans-Mississippi West were not a major factor for the Confederacy, but Union control would inhibit their movement and the flow of large-scale Southern military units. Midwestern farmers could now use the river to export their goods and were solidly behind the Union war effort. With the north-south axis secure, Grant was free to attempt to split the Confederacy from west to east.

NOTES

1. David D. Porter, *Naval History of the Civil War* (1886; reprint ed., Secaucus, NJ: Castle Books, 1984), 178.

2. Bradley S. Osbon and Albert Bigelow Paine, *A Soldier of Fortune: Personal Memoirs of Captain B. S. Osbon* (New York: McClure, Phillips and Co., 1906), 185.

3. Ibid., 188.

4. Porter, *Naval History of the Civil War*, 181.

5. *ORN*, series 1, vol. 18 (Washington, DC: Government Printing Office, 1894), 769.

6. George Dewey, *Autobiography of George Dewey: Admiral of the Navy* (New York: Scribner, 1913), 63–64.

7. Ibid., 64–65.

8. Osbon and Paine, *A Soldier of Fortune*, 192.

9. *ORN*, series 1, vol. 18:306.

10. Dewey, *Autobiography*, 68–69.

11. *ORN*, series 1, vol. 18:344.

CHAPTER FOUR

THE SIEGE OF CHARLESTON

WHILE U.S. NAVY FORCES were engaged in securing the great western rivers, Union naval commanders were intensifying their blockade of the Confederacy's coasts. Although by June 1863 Union warships had intercepted 885 blockade runners, it was impossible to catch all of them. The blockade became a major business in which specially built ships operated out of Nassau in the Bahamas, Havana in Cuba, Bermuda, and Halifax, Nova Scotia. With prices in the South soaring to astronomical heights, the blockade could be incredibly lucrative for those who were successful. Charleston and Wilmington became the principal points of entry for the blockade runners, and Union strategists believed that they could be closed only by actual occupation.

The great Southern port of Charleston, fount of the Rebellion—the Ordinance of Secession had been signed and the first shots of the war fired there—became a symbol for both sides. The Union siege of Charleston ended up being the longest campaign of the war. It and the later operations against Wilmington certainly were not commensurate in cost with what might have been achieved there in a military or naval sense, but the battles were undertaken primarily for political reasons. Northern leaders believed that taking Charleston would be a great blow to the South's morale, but they seem to have ignored the effects that a Northern failure would have had on both North and South.

The commander of the South Atlantic Blockading Squadron, Rear Adm. Samuel F. Du Pont, had urged army leaders to continue on against Charleston immediately after the capture of Port Royal, but they had refused. Du Pont continued to believe that the only way the city could be taken was through a combined land-sea assault. Utilizing their base at Port Royal, Union forces first attempted to block the harbor physically, with what the

Confederates derided as the "Stone Fleet," hulks filled with rocks and scuttled to obstruct the main channel. But these were soon washed away by the powerful tides and storms.

Union forces then attempted to mount a naval operation against the city. Welles and leaders in Washington believed that the city might be taken by naval assault alone—that naval forces might simply rush past Fort Sumter, rather than attempt to batter it into submission. Once beyond Sumter, the powerful guns of the Union ironclads would force the Confederates to withdraw from their other forts and James Island. They reasoned that Charleston would surrender, just as New Orleans had yielded to Farragut. Assistant Secretary of the Navy Fox particularly saw this as a chance for the navy to win glory, with the army sitting by as a spectator. In any case, a joint operation would require many more men than the ten thousand troops under Union Maj. Gen. David Hunter at Hilton Head, and additional forces were not available given the demands of the concurrent Vicksburg and Gettysburg Campaigns. If Charleston was to be attacked and taken, it would have to be by the navy alone.

Du Pont knew better. Charleston had been continually strengthened, and by 1862 the city certainly was the Southern city best able to withstand an attack from the sea. Its defenses involved a mix of land-based artillery, new technology such as torpedoes and submersible vessels, obstructions to block river and harbor approaches, and prepared positions into which the relatively small numbers of Confederate troops available could be shifted on short notice. By 1863, Charleston boasted a three-tiered defensive system. This system consisted of an outer layer on the Atlantic barrier islands astride the mouth of the harbor, along with the central position of Fort Sumter to cover the channel; a second layer of artillery batteries in the inner harbor to take under fire any Federal ships that broke through; and a third layer of land forts to protect the flanks, the way by which the British had taken the city in 1780 during the American Revolution.

In their efforts to take Charleston the Federals relied on ironclads. Certainly, U.S. Secretary of the Navy Gideon Welles, Washington officials, and much of Northern public opinion came to believe that the numerous ironclad monitors and *New Ironsides*, the most powerful ironclad in the U.S. Navy, could not fail to smash their way into the harbor.

Rear Admiral Du Pont did not share the confidence of his superiors; indeed, he had shown a marked reluctance to attack either Charleston or Fort Sumter. Under continued prodding from Welles, however, he agreed to try. Du Pont, of course, enjoyed the advantage of a sound familiarity with the obstacles that stood in his path. The current and hydrography as much as the man-made defenses conspired against an attacker. The currents could run 3 to 5 knots, which was quite fast. Also, the shallows of Charleston Bar blocked direct entrance to the harbor. There were irregular breaks in the bar, all of which joined at the entrance. Deep-draft ships could use the Main Ship, Swash, and North Channels, but only light-draft vessels could use the rightmost Maffitt's Channel (also known as Sullivan's Island Channel), which in any case ran hard against Fort Sullivan. Navigating all this in peacetime was difficult; now it was much more perilous because the defenders had removed buoys marking the channels. The wide and deep Main Ship Channel was the only safe approach for an attacker.

The man-made obstacles to an attacker consisted of power-ful defensive works. To the left of the harbor entrance lay Morris Island, with Fort Wagner and Battery Gregg. Immediately ahead, and just inside the harbor entrance, was the pentagon-shaped Fort Sumter, while to the left of the main entrance was Sullivan's Is-land and its principal fort, Fort Moultrie, along with Batteries Bee and Beauregard. An attacking naval force reaching the har-bor mouth would be vulnerable to fire from three sides: Battery Gregg, Fort Sumter, and Fort Moultrie.

Charleston's inner defenses against attack from the sea con-sisted of Fort Johnson and Battery Glover on James Island, Fort Ripley and Castle Pinckney in the harbor itself, and the White Point Battery (Battery Ramsay) in Charleston. Sumter, made of brick, and Moultrie, of masonry-faced earth, were the two most powerful works in the defensive system. All save Sumter were earthworks or masonry-clad earthworks, low lying and difficult to destroy by naval gunfire.

As Du Pont prepared for an assault, he demanded more iron-clads, writing that "the limit of my wants in the need of ironclads is the capacity of the [Navy] Department to supply them."[1] The department endeavored to meet his requests and ultimately sent him all but one of its new monitor ironclads. By the spring of 1863, however, Welles was impatient and was comparing Du Pont in his caution to General McClellan.

Du Pont's hesitancy was not just over the number of ironclads he would have available in an assault but also over mechanical problems of the monitors and growing doubts about their ability to destroy shore fortifications. He selected Fort McAllister on the Ogeechee River, Georgia, as a test. This earthwork mounted eight or nine guns. On January 27, 1863, Du Pont sent Commander John L. Worden in the *Passaic*-class monitor *Montauk*, accompanied by the gunboats *Seneca*, *Wissahickon*, and *Dawn*, and the mortar schooner *C. P. Williams* to attack McAllister. The *Montauk* was unable to get in close to the fortification because of sunken obstacles that appeared to be protected by torpedoes. The monitor mounted two Dahlgren smoothbores—1 x 15-inch and 1 x 11-inch. These guns blasted away at Fort McAllister for four hours but without noticeable effect. Worden noted that Confederate return fire was quite accurate—his ship was struck fourteen times—but the monitor suffered no damage from it.

Learning on January 28 from a runaway slave the position of the torpedoes that had blocked the *Montauk*'s way the day before, on February 1, Du Pont sent Worden back to Fort McAllister, with the *Montauk* and her same consorts. This time the *Montauk* was able to move within six hundred yards of the fort. Both sides fired rather accurately, the monitor taking forty-eight hits in the course of the four-hour engagement. Although the Union vessel was not seriously damaged, the Confederate fort was still defiant.

The *Montauk*'s unsatisfactory forays clearly worried Du Pont, who wrote: "If one ironclad cannot take eight guns, how are five to take 147 guns in Charleston harbor?"[2] As Du Pont contemplated the situation on January 31, Confederate Flag Officer Duncan N. Ingraham, under cover of morning fog, sortied from Charleston to attack ten unarmored Union vessels of the blockading squadron lying just off the harbor. Ingraham used the casemated ironclad rams *Palmetto State* (Commander John Rutledge) and *Chicora* (Commander John R. Tucker). The *Palmetto State* closed on the Union blockader *Mercedita* (Capt. Henry S. Stellwagen) without being detected, and the *Mercedita* was unable to depress her guns sufficiently to fire on her opponent. On being rammed and fired on, the *Mercedita* surrendered in a sinking state. Meanwhile, *Chicora* closed on the *Keystone State* (Commander William E. LeRoy) and hit her ten times, disabling her machinery and setting her on fire. A quarter of the *Keystone State*'s crew were casualties: twenty men dead and a like number wounded. The *Augusta*, *Quaker City*, and *Memphis* then came to the rescue.

Although she had two feet of water in her hold and was leaking badly, the *Keystone State* survived. Lt. Commander Pendleton Watmough's *Memphis* towed her out of the action while the other Union gunboats engaged the rams. Both the *Quaker City* and *Augusta* were damaged in the exchange of fire, although not severely. The Union screw sloop *Housatonic* (Capt. William R. Taylor) brought the rams under fire and chased them back into Charleston Harbor. Charleston's commander, Gen. P. G. T. Beauregard, claimed that the blockade was broken, but despite the damage inflicted by the rams, that was not the case.

The *Montauk* returned to Fort McAllister on February 28. This time, Worden intended to destroy the Confederate cruiser *Nashville*. Seized and converted from a passenger steamer at Charleston at the beginning of the war, the *Nashville* had been active in European waters from November 1861 to February 1862 and had taken two prizes. In 1862 she had been converted into a blockade runner, and for nearly nine months she had been waiting for an opportunity to run the blockade. The *Nashville* was now aground in the Ogeechee River near the fort, and on the 28th the *Montauk*'s shells set her on fire and destroyed her at 1,200-yards' range. The monitor was hit in return five times from the fort but without material result. However, the *Montauk* was badly damaged by the explosion of a torpedo under her hull, the effects of which took several weeks to repair.

The extreme vulnerability of the monitors to this type of defensive weapon was shown by the sinking of the *Weehawken* off Charleston. She went down on December 6, 1863, as the result of an undiscovered leak. With only about five minutes from the time the alarm was given to the sinking, thirty-one men drowned. On January 16, 1865, *Patapsco* struck a torpedo while in the Charleston River off Fort Sumter and went down within one minute.

Fort McAllister certainly received its share of attention. On March 3, Du Pont sent the monitors *Passaic, Patapsco,* and *Nahant* against the fort. They were assisted by the gunboats *Seneca, Wissahickon,* and *Dawn* and three mortar boats. Du Pont intended this action as a test of the new ships, each of which mounted 1 x 15-inch and 1 x 11-inch Dahlgrens in their turret, rather than a serious attempt to take the fort. Capt. Percival Drayton of the *Passaic* reported that while the monitors, as before, were practically unscathed by the fort's fire, little or no damage had been done to the fort, certainly nothing that could not be repaired overnight.

As Du Pont feared, this lack of destruction merely gave heart to the Confederate defenders of Charleston, who now tended to denigrate the monitors. In spite of the monitors' ability to withstand punishment, it took nearly seven minutes for their 15-inch guns to be readied for firing, thus slowing their paired 11-inch guns to the same rate. The slow rate of fire rendered the monitors incapable of inflicting, in a short span of time, the sort of damage necessary to reduce shore fortifications. This inefficiency of fire would be especially crippling to the Union side in any attempt at Charleston, given the time necessary to get into position.

During the first week in April the remaining monitors arrived for Du Pont's forces. With no army reinforcements available, he resigned himself to a naval assault alone. Du Pont chose as his flagship the *New Ironsides*, certainly the most powerful ship in the U.S. Navy and the best suited of all the vessels for shore bombardment, save for her deep draft and relative lack of maneuverability. Her wooden spar deck was vulnerable to plunging fire, and her captain took steps to protect it by the addition of sandbags. Barricades of sandbags also were installed below decks to protect against the effects of raking fire from bow or stern. Du Pont understood the risks of an assault from inside the harbor. Attackers would have to navigate around numerous obstacles in the channel; should a ship become hung up on one of these obstacles, it would be easy prey for destruction by the shore batteries.

Torpedoes also posed a significant threat, which was partially met by a new device, known from its appearance as a "boot-jack." Invented by Ericsson, it consisted of a raft shaped to fit around the bow of a monitor and pushed ahead by her. It was equipped with grapnels to snare any torpedoes. Ericsson planned to place at the end of each raft a torpedo that would be detonated when it came into contact with an obstacle, destroying it. This design, however, was eliminated for fear that it would endanger other vessels. This raft was the only counter-torpedo device available. Still another problem was the deep draft of the *New Ironsides*. Mounting sixteen heavy guns, she had something approaching half of Du Pont's artillery. Despite these difficulties, Du Pont decided to attack from inside the harbor. Doing so would distance his ships from Fort Moultrie, provide deeper water for maneuvering, and place his ships where he believed that certain of the Confederate forts could not fire on them.

The Confederate defenders, although they were mistaken in their expectations of a joint army-navy assault, nonetheless had Du Pont's basic plan figured out. They expected the Union monitors to run to several hundred yards from Fort Sumter, where they would be protected from the parapet and upper guns of the fort, and then attempt to breach the fort. Du Pont planned to run past the outer defenses and Sumter. Instead of continuing on to attack Charleston, he would try to destroy Sumter from the north and northwest. Capt. John Rodgers of the *Weehawken* suggested Du Pont be close enough to breach the walls with the ironclads' powerful guns, yet far enough away to render the fort's guns largely ineffective against the ironclads. British experiments indicated that ironclads were relatively safe from return fire at a range of twelve hundred to thirteen hundred yards. Rodgers suggested that the ironclads anchor to improve their accuracy of fire and be safe from torpedoes. Du Pont, however, preferred an attack at closer range, even if it increased the risks to his ships, to enhance the accuracy of his relatively small number of guns.

Du Pont planned a daylight attack. Charleston's commander, General Beauregard, wrote after the fact that night attacks would have rendered the ironclads much more difficult to hit and would have been successful over a two- to three-day period. But this observation did not take into account the difficulty of maneuvering the ironclads at night in the tricky current.

Du Pont's strategy was to cross the bar with seven monitors, the *New Ironsides*, and the hybrid *Keokuk*. Once across, the monitor

Weehawken, commanded by Captain Rodgers, would lead the other ships up the Main Ship Channel. The flagship would be fifth in line. The *New Ironsides* was the largest ship in the squadron; in the middle of the formation, her signal flags could be more easily seen, but her deep draft meant that she would have to remain in the middle of the channel, thus precluding Du Pont from veering out of the line to take the lead. He would have to rely on Rodgers's judgment. The *Keokuk* would be last in line.

The Union ships were not to return fire from the batteries on Morris Island but would instead steam into the harbor and then open fire against Sumter, without anchoring, at the close range of six hundred to eight hundred yards from the northwest face of the fort. After Sumter had been reduced, Du Pont planned to have the ironclads concentrate on shelling the Morris Island forts.

The ironclads were to cross Charleston Bar on April 5, but this maneuver was put off until the next morning. Because of delays and poor visibility, Du Pont scheduled the attack for April 7. The Confederate defenders were well aware of Union preparations and what lay ahead.

On the 7th a morning haze soon burned off, but on the urging of his principal pilot, Du Pont agreed to delay the attempt until the ebb tide to facilitate spotting obstructions in the water. At 12:10 P.M., Du Pont ordered signals raised for the squadron to get under way at one cable's length of two hundred yards. By 1:00 the ships were all moving up the channel, despite difficulty in maintaining their positions in the fast-moving current. *Weehawken* had problems with the torpedo raft; in the rise and fall of the seaway, the two structures worked against each other, causing damage.

At 2:10 the *Weehawken* encountered the first Confederate obstructions across the channel from Fort Sumter northeastward to Fort Moultrie. These obstacles consisted of a series of buoys supporting a tangled mass of rope. Respected as a bold commander, Rodgers inspected the obstacles; but instead of plowing through the rope obstruction across the channel or trying the grapnel-equipped torpedo-clearing raft, he turned aside. This maneuver avoided the probability of fouling his propeller and holding the monitor in position for an indefinite period under the guns of the Confederate forts, but it threw the remainder of the Union

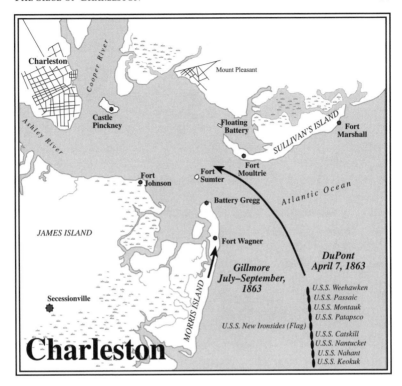

line into further confusion. It also meant the end of Du Pont's plan of running past the point with the heaviest concentration of Confederate firepower.

The obstacles had done their work, delaying the lead Union warship, hence all others. At about 3:00 nearly one hundred Confederate guns and mortars opened up on the Union line with the *Weehawken* only about seven hundred yards away from Sumter. About fifteen minutes later, Du Pont signaled to begin the action. The Union ships commenced shelling the east and northeast faces of Fort Sumter, but they made no effort to try and pass the rope obstruction.

The battle went on at ranges between 550 and 800 yards for nearly 2 hours. With only about a foot of water under her keel, the *New Ironsides* was soon in trouble, and the monitors *Catskill* and *Nantucket*, which were astern of her, collided with the flagship.

The *Keokuk* also ran past the flagship and soon was in great difficulty. In short order the battle scene was covered in smoke so thick that crews had problems seeing their target of Fort Sumter; visibility from the flagship was only about 50 yards.

U.S. Navy bombardment of Fort Sumter, April 7, 1863. From *Harper's Weekly* 7 (January–June 1863): 285. Naval Historical Center. NH 59274

Far from pounding the Confederate forts into submission, the ships themselves sustained some four hundred hits, which heavily damaged a number of the monitors. The *Keokuk* was the hardest hit. Protected by 4-inch iron armor laid on edgeways, 1 inch apart with intervening spaces being filled with wood, she proved quite vulnerable to enemy fire. Running ahead of the crippled *Nahant* and to avoid fouling her in the narrow channel, the *Keokuk* came within about six hundred yards of Fort Sumter's guns and remained there some thirty minutes. She was hit some ninety times, nineteen shots piercing her at or below the waterline. Sixteen crew members were wounded, including her captain, Commander Alexander C. Rhind. Having difficulty keeping the *Keokuk* afloat, Rhind withdrew from action at about 4:40 and anchored overnight beyond the range of Confederate guns.

Du Pont broke off the action at dusk, after about two hours of bombardment. Because of their relatively small number of guns, the Union ships had fired a total of only 139 rounds; the Confederate shore guns, meanwhile, had fired 2,229. Casualties were slight on both sides. The Confederates suffered 4 dead or mortally wounded and 10 lesser injuries. The Union side had 1 mortally wounded and 22 lesser injuries. But these numbers could not mask the fact that the Confederates had beaten back a major Union effort and gained a stunning victory.

Du Pont initially reported to Welles that he had intended to resume the battle the next day, but the commanders of the ironclads then presented their damage reports to the admiral. The *Keokuk*'s crew was trying to keep her afloat; the *Passaic* had suffered the second-most damage. Her 11-inch Dahlgren was disabled, the top of the pilothouse was loosened, and armor bolt had been broken. The *Nantucket* had been hit fifty-one times, and her 15-inch gun could not fire on account of a disabled port shutter. The *Nahant*'s turret was jammed; the *Patapsco*'s heavy gun was out of action because one of the bolts in a cap-square that held it in place on its mount was fractured. Other monitors had broken plates and other problems. Interestingly, the only non-monitor in the action, *New Ironsides*, had taken more than sixty hits but had no serious damage. Although Union engineers worked during the night to repair the monitors, Du Pont became convinced that another attack would have turned "a failure into a disaster." He reported to Welles that five of the ironclads were "wholly or partially disabled after a brief engagement."[3]

The *Keokuk*'s crew was able to keep the ironclad afloat that night only because the water was calm. Despite assistance from the tug *Dandelion*, she sank the next day when a wind came up. At 7:40 A.M., Commander Rhind ordered the crew to abandon ship. She went down at 8:20, only her funnels remaining above water. The Union had lost one of its prized ironclads.

Du Pont now declared that Charleston could not be taken by naval attack alone. He feared the Confederates might sink and then salvage one of his monitors, with the possibility that the whole coast might be lost. Claiming that he had never advised the attack on Charleston, he withdrew his monitors to Port Royal, leaving the *New Ironsides* as the sole ironclad on station off Charleston. This "guardian of the blockade," as she came to be called, there performed yeoman service over the next months.

Du Pont's prudent position regarding another attack on Charleston became widely known and was mistakenly perceived in Washington and by much of the Northern press as defeatism. Soon there were calls for his removal. After some deliberation, Welles replaced Du Pont at Charleston with Rear Adm. Andrew H. Foote. But Foote died in New York City at the end of June of Bright's disease while on his way to take up his new command.

Reluctantly, Welles turned to the navy's leading ordnance expert, Rear Adm. John Dahlgren. Dahlgren ruthlessly had exploited his ordnance achievements and close relationship with Lincoln to secure promotion to admiral and then to obtain a seagoing command. Much resentment existed among senior navy commanders over Dahlgren's appointment, for he lacked experience at sea. Whether from ambition or a desire to prove his critics wrong, or both, Dahlgren lobbied for the command and secured it. He took up his post as commander of the South Atlantic Blockading Squadron on July 6.

Before Dahlgren arrived, another major ironclad battle took place in Wassaw Sound, Georgia. On June 17, 1863, the Confederate ironclad *Atlanta*, under Commander William A. Webb, accompanied by the wooden steamers *Isondiga* and *Resolute*, sallied to engage the *Passaic*-class monitors, *Weehawken* under Captain Rodgers and *Nahant* under Commander John Downes. The *Atlanta* mounted 2 x 6.4-inch and 2 x 7-inch rifled guns. The 6-inch guns were in broadside mounts, while the 7-inchers were on pivot mounts to be able to fire to either side. She also had a percussion spar torpedo fitted to her bow that Webb hoped to explode against the *Weehawken*.

But the *Atlanta* grounded in coming out, and although gotten off, she failed to obey her helm. The monitors *Weehawken* and *Nahant* then worked in close to the Confederate ironclad, with Rodgers waiting until the *Weehawken* was only about three hundred yards away to open fire. The Union monitor, armed with 1 x 11-inch and 1 x 15-inch Dahlgren smoothbores, fired just five shots in fifteen minutes at relatively close range. Four of these struck, smashing through the *Atlanta*'s armored casemate, disabling her guns, causing personnel casualties, and forcing her to surrender. The next year the *Atlanta* was incorporated into the U.S. Navy.

From July to September 1863, Dahlgren kept up a naval bombardment of the Charleston defenses, this time in cooperation with land attacks by troops under Maj. Gen. Quincy Adams Gillmore. A brilliant young engineer, Gillmore had finished first in his class at West Point and made his reputation in the April 1862 bombardment and capture of Fort Pulaski, Georgia. Gillmore was convinced he could replicate this success against both Forts Wagner and Sumter at Charleston. On July 10, Dahlgren's ships supported Gillmore in crossing nearly three thousand troops to the south end of Morris Island and advancing them to within one-half mile of Fort Wagner. During this operation the monitors *Catskill* (flagship under Commander George W. Rodgers), *Nahant*, *Montauk*, and *Weehawken* dueled with Fort Wagner for nearly twelve hours. Meanwhile, Union troops dug trenches forward that allowed them to position Parrott guns within range of both Confederate positions. For the next two months the navy supported the army effort ashore, mounting no fewer than twenty-five separate attacks to assist the effort to capture the remainder of Morris Island.

On August 17, able to position a number of heavy guns to shell Sumter, Gillmore began a week-long bombardment of that fort, again supported by ironclads. On the 23rd, Dahlgren mounted a night ironclad attack against Sumter. He repeated this at close range on September 1, the monitors suffering but little damage in the exchange. Still, Sumter held.

Gillmore now prepared to fire against Charleston. By the existing rules of warfare the city was a legitimate target. A fortified city, it was also home to war industries, and it sheltered blockade runners. But the Union drive to take Charleston ran deeper than that.

On August 21, Gillmore sent General Beauregard a demand for the evacuation of Fort Sumter and Morris Island within four hours and said that if this evacuation was not carried out he would open fire on Charleston. With no immediate response forthcoming, at 1:30 A.M. on August 22, Union shells began falling on Charleston. The chief weapon used was the "Swamp Angel," a large 200-pounder Parrott rifled gun that, before it burst, sent three dozen shells into the waterfront district of the city, setting fires and causing no little panic.

Fort Wagner, the principal Union target, repulsed several attacks with heavy Union losses. Finally, on September 6, as a result of Union sapping operations, the Confederates abandoned Wagner, and Union troops promptly occupied it. Its loss greatly diminished Charleston as a haven for blockade runners.

On September 7, Dahlgren mounted a major attack on Sumter using the monitors *Passaic, Patapsco, Lehigh, Nahant, Montauk*, and *Weehawken*. The monitors drew little fire in return, save from Fort Moultrie on Sullivan's Island. The *Weehawken*, however, grounded in the pass between Fort Sumter and Cummings Point, and all the Union ships were subjected to heavy attack at daybreak from the shore batteries. Dahlgren called in the *New Ironsides* to cover the stranded *Weehawken*. She anchored some twelve hundred yards from Fort Moultrie, engaging it and driving the gunners to cover. She fired 483 shells and was struck at least seventy times in return, although not seriously damaged. The *New Ironsides* finally had to withdraw when she had expended all her 11-inch ammunition. Finally, that afternoon the *Weehawken* was at last refloated, and all the Union ships withdrew. The *Passaic* had been hit ninety times and her turret disabled.

Dahlgren noted during these operations that Sumter appeared to be partly evacuated, and he ordered a boat attack from Morris Island. Commander Thomas H. Stevens led the attack on the night of September 8–9 by some four hundred sailors and marines in more than thirty boats. The Confederates were waiting. Alerted to the Union plan as a consequence of the recovery of a signal key from the wreck of the *Keokuk*, they waited until the boats were nearly ashore before opening fire with guns, small arms, and hand grenades. The Confederate ironclad *Chicora* provided enfilading fire. More than one hundred Union prisoners were taken.

All the ironclads now needed extensive repairs at Port Royal, and their condition marked the end of active Union operations against Charleston for some weeks while repairs were accomplished. Although Union ships and troops ashore continued to keep up operations during September to December 1863, the other Confederate forts continued to hold out. The Confederates shifted heavy guns from Sumter to the more powerful works of Moultrie and Jackson, and they continued to develop torpedoes and other devices.

A frustrated Dahlgren wanted to press the attack. Believing that an effort to pass through the line of piling that constituted the second obstruction would mean the loss of some ships, he requested additional monitors from Washington. But the Navy Department demurred in line with experience, reluctant to have its sole ironclad squadron "incur extreme risks." Thus ended the effort to run monitors into Charleston Harbor and shell the city into submission.

Charleston fell only in February 1865, after Maj. Gen. William T. Sherman's troops had cut the city's land communications with the rest of the South. Indeed, after the failure of the 1863 Union naval assault, the Confederates provided additional incentive for the Union ships not to renew the assault as they attempted to dislodge the blockade with new defensive weapons of their own.

Traditionally, a weaker naval power endeavors to offset a superior opponent at sea with new and improved weapons. The Confederacy did make a major effort to acquire powerful seagoing ships in Europe. The most important were two turreted warships ordered from the Lairds of Birkinhead in England. Known as the Laird rams, these two ships each mounted two Cowper Coles-designed turrets, superior to the Ericsson turret, which were carried high in the ship. The ships were protected with 5-inch armor on the turrets (10 inches on the faces) and 3- to 4.5-inch armor on the sides. Although they were supposedly under construction for Egypt with the code names *El Monassir* and *El Tousson*, it became clear that the two were intended for the Confederacy, and, with the war having shifted decisively in favor of the Union, the British government stepped in and seized them in October 1863. Intended to be the *Mississippi* and *North Carolina*, they were purchased for the Royal Navy in February 1864 and commissioned in October 1865 as the *Scorpion* and *Wyvern*. In Royal Navy service each turret mounted 2 x 9-inch rifled guns. Had they been turned over to the Confederacy, these two ships might have destroyed the Union fleet.

Mallory also wanted to purchase ironclads on the Continent. Only one of these, the *Stonewall*, reached Confederate hands. First of a two-ship class built in France, her sister was unnamed and never completed. Laid down in 1863 and known by her cover name of *Sphinx*, she was launched in June 1864. The previous February, Paris decided that she would not be given to the Confederacy and arranged for her sale to Denmark instead. Renamed the *Staerkodder*, she was intended for service in Denmark's 1864 war with Prussia and Austria. But when the Danes were defeated, Copenhagen refused her and she was returned to France as the *Olinde*. The French builders were able to arrange her transfer to the Confederacy, and she was commissioned at sea. Fitted with a pronounced ram bow, she was armed with three muzzle-loading rifled guns: 1 x 11-inch 300-pounder and 2 x 5-inch. The *Stonewall* departed Ferrol, Spain, on March 25, 1865, and made it as far as Cuba, where her crew learned in May that the Civil War was over. Later she joined the Imperial Japanese Navy as the *Adzuma*.

The Confederacy also made extensive strides to develop underwater warfare as a means to offset the vast Union advantage in ships. The South had employed land mines as early as the 1862 peninsula campaign. When Confederate troops withdrew from Yorktown that May, they left behind artillery shells in the roads, rigged to explode if stepped on. At the time such activity was considered quite controversial and outside the bounds of civilized warfare, but as the war increased in destructiveness, such prohibitions were ignored. Many Southern strategists came to see mines as a means of reducing the Union naval advantage; influential Confederate Navy commander and scientist Matthew F. Maury was an early proponent of mines and conducted extensive experiments with them.

Civil War naval mines/torpedoes were of several types. Either scratch-built or constructed from barrels as casings, they essentially were stationary weapons, a sort of buoy held in place at an appropriate distance from the surface by a cable anchored to the sea bottom by a weight. Positioned in rivers or harbors to explode against the hulls of Union warships, the mines had two basic types of detonation: by contact and by electricity. The first type was detonated when "horns" surrounding the charge were broken, setting off a chemical reaction that ignited the charge; the second was fired by electrical connections from batteries on shore. The first type was more certain to explode, but, because they were unable to distinguish their victim, they were dangerous to friendly vessels. The second type could be used only close to shore.

More often than not, such early mines failed to explode as a result of faulty detonating equipment or becoming waterlogged, or they were swept away by the current. Even so, they had a profound psychological effect on sailors aboard ship, producing what was called "torpedo fever" among Union crews.

One of the first uses of torpedoes during the Civil War came during the February 1862 Union assault on Fort Henry on the Tennessee River. The wife of a Confederate captain at the fort inadvertently revealed their presence in a conversation with some Union scouts, and Flag Officer Foote immediately set crews of his lighter gunboats to sweep for them. The mines, sheet-iron cylinders some 5.5 feet long, pointed at the ends, and each containing about seventy-five pounds of gunpowder, were fired by

Depiction of the explosion of a Confederate electronically fired mine close to the USS *Commodore Barney* on the James River, August 5, 1863. Engraving from *The Soldier in Our Civil War*. Naval Historical Center. NH 51932

contact-type detonators. Union sailors used cutters to bring eight of them to the surface. All those recovered were soaked and harmless. On December 12, 1862, however, the 512-ton Union ironclad *Cairo* succumbed to a mine while in the Yazoo River.

Powder charges in Civil War mines ranged from approximately fifty pounds to large mines containing up to a ton of powder. One of the latter type, detonated electrically, sank the 542-ton Union gunboat *Commodore Jones* in the James River on May 6, 1864. She and two other Union vessels were sweeping for mines when the explosion occurred. The mine blew up directly under the converted ferryboat, immediately tearing the ship apart. The explosion claimed some forty lives. A landing party went ashore and captured two of the Confederate torpedomen and the galvanic batteries that had detonated the mine. Jeffries Johnson, one of the Confederates, refused to divulge the location of other torpedoes until he was placed in the bow of the forward Union ship as a sort of personal minesweeper.

During the war, some fifty ships were sunk or damaged by torpedoes, four-fifths of them Union vessels. Torpedoes sank more Union warships during the war than any other means used by the South. Only one Confederate vessel, the *Albemarle*, was lost to a Union torpedo. Indeed, most of the Confederate vessels that succumbed were in fact victims of Confederate torpedoes. Torpedoes also were used offensively. Spar torpedoes were simply mines placed at the end of a spar or pole. The Confederates built a number of craft designed to operate very low in the water and carry spar torpedoes in their bows to attack Union warships.

In the fighting for Charleston the Confederates used both torpedoes and a submarine to attack the Union blockading fleet, sending out a small, 50-foot-long vessel, the *David*. Designed to operate very low in the water, she resembled a submarine but was in fact strictly a surface vessel. Propelled by a steam engine and manned by four men, she mounted a spar torpedo—a mine at the end of a long pole—that contained sixty pounds of powder inside a copper casing.

The Confederates regarded the *New Ironsides* as the principal threat in the Union squadron, and General Beauregard issued orders for the forts to fire on her in preference to the monitors. Now the *David* would attempt to sink her by another method. Commanded by Lt. William T. Glassell, on the night of October 5, 1863, the *David* approached the *New Ironsides*, getting to within fifty yards of her target before she was discovered. Hailed from the Union ship, the crew of the *David* responded with a shotgun blast and then placed its mine.

The *David* torpedo boat, Confederate navy, photographed at Charleston, South Carolina, in 1865. Naval Historical Center. NH 165-C-750

Although the explosion of the spar torpedo next to her hull damaged the *New Ironsides*, she did not sink. The blast also sent up a great wave of water that washed into the *David* and put out the fire in her steam engine. Believing she was sinking, Glassell and two other members of her crew abandoned ship; one of them subsequently returned to the *David*, where the engineer had succeeded in restarting her furnace fire. Glassell and another crewman were captured. The *David* and similar craft made other subsequent attempts against Union ships at Charleston, without success. *David* and its class were not submarines; they merely took in water as ballast to run on the surface in an awash position. Their open hatch, necessary to provide air for the steam engine, invited disaster through swamping, as indeed occurred. The Union also employed spar torpedoes; one sank the 376-ton Confederate ironclad ram *Albemarle* in October 1864.

On January 16, 1865, despite precautionary sweeps by boats with drags and although she had torpedo netting out, the monitor *Patapsco* went down to one or more torpedoes in the channel off Fort Sumter. She sank so rapidly that she took with her sixty-four men, more than half her crew. The largest ship sunk by a mine during the war, however, was the victim of the Confederate submarine, the *H. L. Hunley*. During the American Revolution, David Bushnell had invented a primitive submarine, the *Turtle*, to counter overwhelming British naval strength; thus, it was no surprise that the Confederacy also developed primitive submarines to use against the Union during the Civil War.

As early as March 1862, Robert R. Barrow, James R. McClintock, and Baxter Watson applied for a letter of marque for a submarine craft they owned, named the *Pioneer*. Only about 20' long and intended for a crew of two, it was propelled by a crankshaft turned by her crew. The *Pioneer* was scuttled to prevent its capture when Union forces took New Orleans. Horace L. Hunley, one of the sureties on the *Pioneer*, McClintock, and Watson then went to Mobile, Alabama, to continue experiments. In mid-February 1863 they tested another submarine along the same lines as the first, this one designed for five men and to deliver a spar torpedo. The craft went down in rough water off Fort Morgan, but no lives were lost.

Undaunted, Hunley and his friends built a third submarine. In early August 1863, when Charleston was under heavy Union attack, General Beauregard requested that she be sent there, with large rewards offered for the destruction of Union ships. On August 15 the submarine arrived at Charleston on two covered railroad flat cars.

The *H. L. Hunley* was built from an iron steam boiler with tapered bow and stern sections added. Some 40' in length, 3.5' in breadth at her widest point, and 4' in depth, she resembled a long thin cigar in shape. She was designed for a crew of nine: one man to steer and eight positioned along the length of the center section to power the submarine, which was done by hand-turning a crankshaft that moved the propeller and pushed the craft forward at about 4 knots. The *H. L. Hunley* was to run awash until close to the target, when she would submerge with the aid of rudders. The submarine was difficult to control, and the men needed fresh air, a supply of which was available only when she was awash.

On August 29 the submarine made several practice dives in Charleston Harbor. She was then moored to a steamer. When the steamer unexpectedly moved from the dock, the submarine was drawn against her side and quickly filled with water through her hatch. Five men drowned but three others, including her commander, Lt. John A. Payne, escaped. The *H. L. Hunley* was raised and refitted. Another crew volunteered, but on October 15 the submarine sank again in Charleston Harbor, and Hunley and a crew of seven perished. The submarine was recovered again, and a third crew, commanded by Infantry Lt. George E. Dixon, volunteered to man her.

The *H. L. Hunley*, Confederate navy submarine. Painting by Conrad Wise Chapman in the Museum of the Confederacy. Naval Historical Center. NH 63086

Meanwhile, the commander of the South Atlantic Blockading Squadron, Admiral Dahlgren, issued orders to the fleet, warning of a possible submarine attack and instructing how best to prepare against it. He ordered ships to anchor so as not to allow the passage of a submarine underneath, to deploy boats as well as nets, and to keep boat howitzers ready, along with a searchlight for each monitor.

The *H. L. Hunley*'s destructive force came in the form of a spar torpedo, possibly designed by General Beauregard. Mounted to the bow, the spar held the torpedo, which terminated in a barbed lance head. When the submarine drove toward its victim, the spar's barb would lodge into the timbers below the water-line. The submarine would then back off, exploding the torpedo by means of a long lanyard.

On the night of February 17, 1864, the *H. L. Hunley* set out and approached the 1,934-ton screw sloop *Housatonic*. The sloop was prepared for such an attack; Capt. Charles Pickering had six lookouts posted, steam in the engine room was up, and crewmen were ready to slip the ship's cable at a moment's notice. At about 9:00 P.M., lookouts on the *Housatonic* spotted the *H. L. Hunley*'s two hatches above water, along with her slight wake, but she was only about seventy-five to one hundred yards from the ship, and it was too late for anything save small arms fire to be directed against her. About three minutes after the submarine was detected and as the sloop was getting under way, the *H. L. Hunley*'s 130-pound spar torpedo exploded. The *Housatonic* became the first ship sunk by a submarine in the history of warfare. Only five of her crew were lost; most simply climbed into the rigging to await rescue. The unstable *H. L. Hunley* survived the blast that sank her victim long enough to signal by lantern that she was return-ing to land, but, probably damaged in the explosion, she sank shortly thereafter.

The Union also experimented with submarines. Among these was a one-man submarine designed by Maj. Edward B. Hunt of the Army Corps of Engineers. While testing his "submarine bat-tery" at the Brooklyn Navy Yard, Hunt died of carbon dioxide poisoning on October 2, 1863. Union submarines did not take to the sea during the war, however.

NOTES

1. Du Pont to Gustavus Fox, March 2, 1863, in Samuel F. Du Pont, *Samuel Francis Du Pont: A Selection from His Civil War Letters*, 3 vols., ed. John D. Hayes (Ithaca, NY: Cornell University Press, 1969), 2:463.

2. Du Pont to Benjamin Gerhard, January 30, 1863, ibid., 2:394.

3. Du Pont to Gideon Welles, April 8, 1863, *ORN*, series 1, vol. 14 (Washington, DC: Government Printing Office, 1902), 3–4.

CHAPTER FIVE

CONFEDERATE COMMERCE RAIDING

LEADERS OF THE CONFEDERACY attempted to offset the numerical advantage of the U.S. Navy by developing new weapons but they also tried to counter the Union blockade by sending out ships on the high seas against the U.S. merchant marine. The twin pillars of Secretary Mallory's naval policy were securing ironclads and commerce raiding. Americans had enjoyed great success in sending large numbers of privately owned warships to sea against the British in both the American Revolution and the War of 1812. The U.S. Navy as well had largely devoted itself to such a *guerre de course* (war against commerce) in both conflicts. For the Confederacy the situation was analogous to these earlier American wars: a nation weak on the seas faced a far more powerful foe with a formidable fleet but an extensive and vulnerable merchant marine.

Mallory reasoned that if the Confederacy were able to strike a strong blow at Union merchant shipping, it would wound the North financially and might weaken Northern resolve. Even modest successes would force up insurance rates and create economic problems for Northern merchants, perhaps forcing them to bring pressure on Washington for a negotiated end to the war. In any case, even a few such warships would force Washington to dissipate its naval assets, shifting vessels from blockade duties to protect its merchantmen and hunt down the raiders.

The Confederate war against Union commerce began early in the conflict. On April 17, 1861, President Davis had invited applications for letters of marque and reprisal, an action confirmed by the Confederate Congress on May 6. Lincoln's threat that anyone attacking a U.S. vessel would be treated as a pirate did not deter numerous applications for letters of marque from Southern cities and as far away as Great Britain.

The few Confederate privateers that got to sea in May initially found easy hunting. On May 16 the Confederate privateer *Calhoun* took the Union merchant ship *Ocean Eagle* off the Mississippi River's mouth. By the 29th the *Calhoun* had taken four other Union prizes, and two other privateers working with her had taken four other Union ships.

Typical of the privateers was the fast schooner *Savannah*. At only fifty-three tons, with a crew of twenty men, she was armed with only one short 18-pounder of War of 1812 vintage. Carrying the first letter of marque issued by the Confederacy and commanded by Harrison Baker, the *Savannah* departed Charleston on June 2, 1861. She soon captured a merchant brig, the first prize taken by a Charleston privateer, and sent her into port. At dusk the *Savannah* spotted a brig and ran toward her. She turned out to be the U.S. Navy warship *Perry*, mounting 6 x 32-pounders and 1 x 12-pounder howitzer. The *Savannah* had lost part of her top rigging in a storm the night before and thus could not hope to outrun the Union ship. Baker ordered the *Savannah*'s remaining sails lowered to try to avoid detection in the approaching darkness, but she was spotted nonetheless. Both sides subsequently opened fire, their gun flashes illuminating the scene. Heavily outclassed in armament, the *Savannah* was soon forced to surrender. Following her capture, the *Savannah* became something of a *cause célèbre*. Washington labeled her crew as "pirates" and threatened them with the death penalty. Confederate President Davis promptly intervened, threatening to hang Union officers on a one-for-one basis. The North then backed down.

Other Confederate privateers were taken later, some of them at sea and others by cutting-out operations where Union forces went into a harbor and took the vessel by storm. Still others were lost to natural causes; the *Jefferson Davis* out of Charleston, however, took nine prizes before she was wrecked off St. Augustine. Union forces ended privateering out of Pamlico Sound when Flag Officer Silas H. Stringham led his squadron there in August. Privateers were not much use in the war. The Union blockade made it difficult for them to bring their prizes into Southern ports, and subsequently, many privateers were simply converted into blockade runners. A number were sunk or captured in the summer of 1862, and most were gone within a year.

To continue the war against Union commerce the Confederacy relied on state-owned commerce raiders. Whereas only a handful took part in the war, they inflicted significant damage. But the cruisers faced a daunting problem: the lack of a secure supply base. As Commander Matthew F. Maury put it, they would not have "a friendly port in the wide world."[1] Maury's fears proved unfounded; despite difficulties, Confederate commerce raiders got the coal and other supplies they needed.

The *Sumter* was the first such raider. The bark-rigged screw steamer ex-*Havana* was a relatively new steamer packet of 437 tons, launched in 1857. She had been used on the New Orleans to Havana route and was capable of 9 to 10 knots sustained speed. Purchased at New Orleans in April 1861, she was converted into a commerce raider. Among alterations, her decks were strengthened to bear the weight of heavy guns and below deck was reconfigured to carry additional crew and provisions. Little could be done about the exposed nature of her machinery, however; most of it was above the waterline and hence vulnerable to enemy fire. Commander Raphael Semmes, a former U.S. Navy lieutenant, had charge of the conversion and became her captain.

Commissioned on June 3, and armed with 1 x 8-inch gun and 2 x 32-pounders, the *Sumter* was typical of her type in that she did most of her cruising under sail. Her fuel capacity was sufficient only for five days' steaming. Easily the most feared and notorious Confederate naval commander, Semmes was an introvert who did not socialize with his officers. His leadership was of the quiet variety but unquestioned. Confederate naval agent in Britain James D. Bulloch had high praise for Semmes's abilities, but outspoken and partisan U.S. Navy Adm. David Porter expressed a contrarian viewpoint. He called Semmes "perhaps the most vindictive of all the officers of the Confederate Navy." Porter also wrote that while in the U.S. Navy, Semmes had "little reputation as an officer."[2]

In fact, Semmes had distinguished himself during the Mexican War. In 1852 he had published the well-received *Service Afloat and Ashore during the Mexican War*, which detailed his war experiences. He argued that if Mexico had fitted out privateers to prey on U.S. shipping, they should have been treated as pirates. Now as a Confederate navy officer, Semmes had urged Mallory to adopt a commerce-raiding strategy.

On June 18, Semmes ran the *Sumter* down to the Mississippi River's mouth to await the right moment to escape the Union blockading squadron and put to sea. On the 30th, taking advantage of the fact that the powerful *Brooklyn* was off station to chase down another vessel, Semmes got the *Sumter* under way. The *Brooklyn* turned as it spotted the tell-tale black smoke of the steamer trying to escape to sea. In what Porter described as "one of the most exciting chases of the war,"[3] the *Sumter* lost valuable time getting past a vessel stranded on the bar. The *Brooklyn* was then only seven miles away, and making 11.5 knots to the *Sumter*'s 9. Before too much longer the gap had closed to four miles, and steam pressure in the *Sumter*'s engines went to dangerous levels. Semmes ordered his men to throw fresh-water casks and even a gun overboard. A fair wind and her fore-and-aft rig, which enabled her to sail close to the wind and yet also use her engine, worked to the *Sumter*'s advantage. Gradually she began to pull away, and after a three-and-one-half-hour pursuit, the *Brooklyn* gave up. The *Sumter* was now free to roam the Gulf. Mallory's orders to Semmes were "do the enemy's commerce the greatest injury in the shortest time."[4]

At first operating in the West Indies, the *Sumter*, on July 3, took her first prize, the *Golden Rocket*, a merchant bark. Unable to get his prizes into port, Semmes destroyed most of them, including the *Golden Rocket*. Over the next six months, Semmes cruised the Caribbean, capturing nine other vessels. He sailed the *Sumter* along the South American coast to Brazil, then back to the West Indies, but he found only two U.S. registered vessels, both of which he burned. The absence of other U.S. vessels convinced Semmes that he would do better in European waters, and he took the *Sumter* into the Atlantic. To try to take the *Sumter*, U.S. Secretary of the Navy Welles weakened the blockade by dispatching the *Niagara*, *Powhatan*, *Keystone State*, *Richmond*, *Iroquois*, and *San Jacinto* in search of her, which led directly to the *Trent* Affair.

On November 8, 1861, while searching for the *Sumter*, overzealous U.S. Navy Capt. Charles Wilkes of the *San Jacinto* put into Havana to coal and learned that Confederate commissioners James M. Mason and John Slidell had sailed recently for England on board the British mail packet *Trent*. Wilkes pursued the *Trent*, caught up with her, and forcibly removed Mason and Slidell.

Much of the North lionized Wilkes for the deed, but British Prime Minister Lord Palmerston threatened war over the incident. Lincoln promptly concluded that one armed conflict at a time was sufficient and resolved what became known as the *Trent* Affair through diplomatic means. Washington disavowed Wilkes's action, and Mason and Slidell were released to the British, although Washington could not resist pointing out to London how this action resembled former Royal Navy impressments.

Late in November, while coaling at St. Pierre, Martinique, the *Sumter* was cornered by the more powerful U.S. Navy screw sloop *Iroquois* (2 x 11-inch Dahlgrens and 4 x 32-pounders), captained by Wilkes. He waited over a week for Semmes to take his ship to sea, but Semmes managed to escape the harbor one night and made for Spain. During the crossing he took six Union prizes.

On January 3 the *Sumter*, in poor condition, put into Cádiz. Spanish authorities allowed Semmes to make only repairs rather than the engine overhaul he wanted. They ordered him to depart and he did so. On the 18th the *Sumter* took two prizes; a day later she arrived at Gibraltar. The British authorities were much more gracious than the Spanish at Cádiz, but the U.S. consul managed to block the sale of coal to the *Sumter*. In the meantime, U.S. Navy warships, including the screw sloop *Kearsarge*, arrived to wait for the raider to come out. Since his ship needed repairs to her boilers and hull for which facilities were not available at Gibraltar, Semmes bowed to the inevitable. With the permission of Confederate commissioner Mason in London, in April he laid up his ship, paid off most of her crew, and left for London, expecting to sail for home from there. In December 1862 the *Sumter* was sold in Gibraltar at auction to a British firm, which put her back into commercial service under the name *Gibraltar*. Semmes was in the process of returning to the Confederacy when he was ordered to England to take command of another commerce raider being built there for the Confederacy.

During the war no fewer than a dozen such ships attacked Union merchantmen. Given the paucity of manufacturing resources and the battles in the South, in May 1861 Secretary Mallory sent naval agents to France and Britain; the most important by far was James Dunwoody Bulloch in Britain. In all, these agents contracted for eighteen vessels, the most successful of which were secured in Britain: the *Alabama*, *Chickamauga*, *Florida*, *Georgia*, *Rappahannock*, *Shenandoah*, and *Tallahassee*. The other eleven ships became blockade runners, were sequestered by the British and French governments, or were not completed by the end of the war. To circumvent neutrality laws, the raiders sailed without armament, which they received elsewhere. It was only a transparent cover, and the British and French governments were well aware of what was going on. London would later pay dearly for its duplicitous role.

Bulloch arrived in England in early June 1861. By adroit maneuvering, he was able to skirt the Foreign Enlistment Act of 1819, which prohibited British citizens from equipping, furnishing, fitting out, or arming any vessel intended for service by foreign belligerent navies. Eminent Liverpool lawyer F. S. Hull assisted Bulloch with the act's intricacies and helped him stay within the letter of the law. Hull maintained that construction of such a ship was not an offense, whatever the intent, and that the offense lay not in the building but in the equipping of such a vessel. Bulloch took care to see that none of the cruisers he had built in Britain went to sea with ordnance, small arms, or warlike stores of any kind. He obtained and shipped armaments in other vessels so that the cruisers could be outfitted in international waters at sea. This maneuver prevented the British government from seizing the two ships.

Within a few weeks of his arrival, Bulloch placed an order with William A. Miller & Sons of Liverpool for construction of the first commerce raider. The firm had considerable experience building wooden ships capable of bearing the heavy weight of ordnance for the Royal Navy. Faecett and Preston & Company, also of Liverpool, built the engines. Supposedly constructed for an Italian buyer and initially known by the cover name of *Otero*, she later was commissioned as CSS *Florida*. The first ships were all of wood, designed as fast sailers but roomy for extended periods at sea. They had to provide adequate space for crew, coal, provisions, and temporary berthing for any captured crew members.

The steam corvette *Florida* was patterned after a Royal Navy dispatch boat but was lengthened to provide more storage space. The greater length also allowed for additional rigging to increase the amount of sail she could carry. Fast, she could make 9.5 knots under steam and 12 under sail.

It was not until January 1862 that the U.S. consul at Liverpool uncovered information as to the true identity of the ship being built there, and Bulloch was able to get the ship to sea before she could be seized. Displacing some 700 tons and powered by one screw, she sailed from Liverpool on March 22 and made for Nassau. Meanwhile, Bulloch also sent out the cargo ship *Bahama* from Scotland with her guns, ammunition, and provisions. At Nassau, Capt. John N. Maffitt took command. But British officials there detained the ship, and Maffitt lost nearly all his 120-man crew. He managed to recruit 20 local seamen and got her to sea as soon as the legal dispute was resolved. The supplies from the *Bahama* were shifted to a local schooner that then followed the *Florida* to sea. Some 75 miles from Nassau, at Green Key, the *Florida* was armed and outfitted. She mounted 2 x 7-inch and 6 x 6-inch rifled guns and a 12-pounder howitzer.

It took a week, but the work was completed by August 17, and the *Florida* was officially placed into service. Unfortunately, much of the crew was down with yellow fever, the scourge of the Tropics. Maffitt had to put into Cardenas, Cuba, for medical help. The situation worsened, however: five men died, including Maffitt's stepson, and were buried at sea; Maffitt himself was near death. The *Florida* then put into Havana, where Maffitt engaged a pilot who knew the entrance to Mobile, the nearest Confederate port.

By keeping close to the Cuban coast, the *Florida* managed to avoid Union warships that were searching for her. Maffitt then made a desperate dash across the Caribbean. On September 4, with only a skeleton crew, the *Florida* arrived off Mobile Bay. There Commander George Preble's squadron of three U.S. Navy ships—screw sloop *Oneida*, screw gunboat *Winona*, and schooner *Rachel Seaman*—blockaded the entrance to the bay. As was so often the case during the war, Preble and Maffitt were old friends, having been shipmates together. Without hesitation and with a full head of steam, Maffitt ran his ship past the Union blockaders. The *Florida* flew an English ensign, and Preble, mindful that another incident similar to the *Trent* Affair might bring war with Britain, hesitated. With the *Florida* about a mile away and bearing down on the *Oneida*, Preble made a major mistake. He reversed his engines to avoid being rammed by what he still believed to be an English vessel. Maffitt continued on course, coming to within eighty yards of the *Oneida* before Preble could get his ship into position to fire a warning shot across the bow of the onrushing vessel.

The captains of the other two Union ships, meanwhile, fully expected the *Oneida* to take care of the situation. Preble fired a second warning shot and then loosed a full broadside at point-blank range. The shots went too high to do serious damage. Maffitt recorded, "Had their guns been depressed, the career of the *Florida* would have ended then and there."[5] At least the broadside alerted the other two Union ships. All three began to fire on the *Florida*.

As shot splashed in the water near the *Florida*, Maffitt ended any doubts as to his ship's identity by ordering the English ensign lowered and the Stars and Bars raised in its place. One 11-inch shell went through the starboard side of her hull close to the waterline, decapitating a fireman and wounding nine other crewmen, before ripping out through the port side and exploding. Had the shell been set to explode a second sooner, the *Florida* would in all probability have been destroyed. Another smaller shell also penetrated the raider's hull. The *Oneida* and *Florida* were close enough that marines on the Union ship were able to fire their muskets. To increase his speed, Maffitt ordered all sails set, but Preble countered by firing grape shot into the raider's rigging, and Maffitt ordered his men to stay below. Maffitt recorded in his diary, "The loud explosions, roar of shot and shell, crashing spars and rigging, mingled with the moans of our sick and wounded, only increased our determination to enter our destined harbor."[6]

Although damaged by the Union cannonade, the *Florida* reached safety, anchoring under the protecting guns of Fort Morgan. This daring escapade enraged Admiral Farragut and led to much unfavorable publicity in the North for the U.S. Navy as well as to increased demands for a tightening of the blockade.

Repairs to the *Florida* were not begun until October 3, when a quarantine on her was lifted. The twin problems that plagued the South throughout the war, a shortage of skilled workers and lack of facilities, delayed completion of the work. The *Florida's* deep draft also created problems and further delay, forcing her to anchor in the bay rather than at Mobile and necessitating shuttling her workers back and forth. Machinery had to be disassembled, shipped to Mobile for repair, and then brought back to the ship for reassembly. Equipment, even rigging, was in short supply, and bad weather also intervened. All these conditions revealed the problems that the Confederacy faced in the naval sphere. Not until January 10, 1863, was the *Florida* again ready for sea.

By then a dozen Union blockaders were in place. Maffitt waited until a dark night, but the *Florida* ran aground in Mobile Bay. It took two days to get her free, and only after her coal and guns had been temporarily removed. The little steamers *Gaines* and *Morgan* then pulled her free. The *Florida* grounded a second time, leading to a repeat of the unloading process. All this probably was fortuitous because the delay brought a storm from the northeast and ideal conditions for an escape attempt.

At 2:00 A.M. on the 17th in a thick mist, the *Florida* got past two blockaders without being detected. She was sighted by the third as a consequence of sparks from her funnel, and Maffitt had the *Florida* raise full steam and set all sails. Making 14.5 knots, she outran her pursuers. Only one threat remained, the *R. R. Culyer*, the only Union warship capable of catching the *Florida*. The Union ship was spotted about 5:00 A.M., only three miles away, and Maffitt ordered all sails stricken and the engines stopped. The sea was rough, and the waves hid the low-lying *Florida* from view.

The *Florida* then cruised the North Atlantic, taking twenty-two merchantmen, including two barks, the *Coquette* and *Lapwing*, which she used as tenders. The *Coquette* was taken at sea on May 6, 1863. Renamed the *Clarence*, she took six prizes before she was burned at sea on June 12, 1863, and her crew transferred to one of her prizes, the *Tacony*, sometimes known as the *Florida No. 2*. The new raider in turn took fifteen prizes before her crew burned her on June 15 and transferred to yet another prize, the *Archer*. The *Lapwing* was carrying a cargo of coal from Boston to Batavia when she was seized on March 28, 1863. Maffitt transferred a howitzer and ammunition to the capture and used her as a tender.

During August 1863 and February 1864 the *Florida* was laid up for repairs at Brest, France. On her second cruise she operated principally off South America, taking another eleven Union merchantmen. In two years of operations, she took thirty-three Union merchant ships and caused an estimated $4,051,000 in damages. The expense of her construction and cruises probably totaled $400,000. On October 4 she put in at the Brazilian port of Bahia to recoal. Three days later the *Florida* was riding at anchor in that port when she was attacked in violation of Brazilian neutrality by the USS *Wachusett*. The Union warship towed her out to sea, and she was sent on to the United States under a prize crew. Anchored at Newport News, Virginia, she was rammed and sunk accidentally on November 28 by the army transport *Alliance*.

The *Alabama* was by far the most successful of the Confederate cruisers, also built in Britain on Bulloch's secret order. During her construction, much discussion ensued concerning the ultimate disposition of "hull 290," later named the *Enrica*. Any trained observer could see that the new ship had been specially designed for speedy conversion into an armed cruiser. The *Enrica* was completed in July 1862.

Bulloch had hoped to take command of the new ship himself, but that honor went to Semmes. On July 30, Bulloch, forewarned that the British government was about to seize the ship, got the *Enrica* to sea. At the same time, Bullock chartered the *Agrippina* to carry the future commerce raider's ordnance, ammunition, stores, and 250 tons of coal. On August 13, Bulloch and Semmes (who had arrived in Liverpool a few days after the *Enrica* sailed) and other officers left Liverpool aboard a third ship, the *Bahama*. All 3 rendezvoused at Porto Praia da Vitória, Terceira, in the Azores on August 9. Portuguese officials were told that the *Enrica* was the *Barcelona*, bound from London to Havana for the Spanish government. On August 24 in international waters, to the tune of "Dixie" and salutes, Semmes commissioned his new command as the *Alabama*. He managed to persuade some 80 of the British seamen in the three ships to sign on as members of her crew. Bulloch then returned to Liverpool with the remaining crewmen and the two other ships. The *Alabama* was on her own.

The *Alabama* was a sleek, three-masted, bark-rigged sloop built of oak with a copper-sheathed hull. Of some nine hundred tons burden, she was 230' x 32' x 20' (in depth). Not without reason, her builder John Laird had boasted that she was the finest of her class in the world. She had a screw propeller powered by two horizontal direct-acting condensing engines and four boilers; her propeller could be detached from the shaft and lifted into a well so that she could make faster speed under sail alone. With her two 300-horsepower engines the *Alabama* was capable of a maximum speed of 13 knots under steam and sail and 10 knots under sail alone.

The *Alabama*, Confederate navy commerce raider, from Lt. Arthur Sinclair, CSN, *Two Years on the Alabama*, 2d ed. (1896). Naval Historical Center. NH 57259

A superb example of the shipbuilder's art, the *Alabama* carried a large spread of canvas high; friend and foe alike could identify her from her exceptionally lofty rigging. The *Alabama* was unusual in that she had a fully equipped machine shop to enable her crew to make all ordinary repairs to her themselves. She carried sufficient coal for eighteen days' continuous steaming, although Semmes preferred to rely on sail when possible. In fact, all but about six of her captures were made under sail alone. If she could reprovision from captured prizes, the *Alabama* would be able to remain at sea a long time.

The *Alabama* was armed with 8 guns: 6 x 32-pounders in broadside and 2 pivot guns amidships—a 100-pounder rifled Blakeley and a smoothbore 8-incher. Her average crew was about

120 men, and she carried 24 officers. Over a 2-year period the *Alabama* traveled an incredible 75,000 miles.

After a brief shakedown cruise the *Alabama* took her first prize vessels in the vicinity of the Azores: American whalers finishing their season there. Her first prize, taken on September 5, was the *Ocmulgee* from Massachusetts, an easy capture. When the *Alabama* came up, the *Ocmulgee* was lying to with a large whale alongside, which her crew was cutting apart. Nonetheless, the *Alabama* approached under false flag. Only when the whaler had replied with the U.S. flag did Semmes order the Confederate ensign hoisted. This tactic remained standard practice throughout the *Alabama*'s life as a commerce raider. Semmes presented his ship as a British or Dutch vessel and even a U.S. Navy warship. Semmes took the *Ocmulgee*'s crew of thirty-seven men on board as well as some of her stores. The next morning he had the prize burned.

In two weeks in the Azores the *Alabama* took and burned ten prizes: eight whalers, one schooner, and one supply ship. After taking off such supplies and merchandise as might be useful for his own crew, Semmes burned the vast majority of the ships he took. On occasion a captured vessel was used for target practice. If land was close, Semmes usually put crews and passengers of his prizes into their ships' boats and they rowed to shore. If no land was nearby, those taken might be kept on board the *Alabama* or their own vessel for a time before being released; others were set free if Semmes was forced to bond their ships. Bonding meant that a captain signed a paper in which he guaranteed to pay a sum, decided in condemnation procedures, to the Confederate government at the end of the war.

Semmes spent two weeks in the Azores, destroying the U.S. whaling industry there. The *Alabama* also weathered a severe storm. Semmes then took his ship west to waters off Newfoundland and New England—the sea-lanes where many Union vessels laden with grain for Europe would pass. Ships taken off the Newfoundland Banks tended to be large and with valuable cargoes. Ironically, destroying vessels carrying wheat to Britain and France was not in Confederate interests. Britain was a net importer of food, and "King Corn" was actually more important to political stability in the British Isles than "King Cotton." Driving up grain prices when there was a European wheat shortage only served to remind London and Paris of the importance of good relations with the North.

During October alone, Semmes took eleven vessels, destroying eight and letting the others go on bond. On the 16th the *Alabama* survived the remnants of a hurricane. Throughout her career she had proved to be an excellent ship in heavy weather.

By now the Northern press and shipowners were demanding that the *Alabama* and other Confederate cruisers be hunted down and destroyed. Although Secretary of the Navy Welles, supported by President Lincoln, assigned top priority to the naval blockade of the Confederacy, more than a dozen Union warships were now searching for the cruiser. They were always a little late or their captains sought the *Alabama* in the wrong location.

While the U.S. Navy was increasingly successful in blockading Confederate ports, it was never able to protect its own merchant marine. Why the major shipping lane between New England and Europe was not better protected is something of a mystery. Semmes sailed the *Alabama* to the Caribbean to meet the tender *Agrippina*. In mid-November he had a narrow escape at Fort de France, Martinique, from the more heavily armed, but decidedly slower, U.S. Navy screw frigate *San Jacinto*. Semmes then took his ship to Blanquilla Island off Argentina to recoal.

Semmes then departed from his mission to destroy Union commercial shipping. Newspapers from a British ship brought information that Union forces had taken Galveston, Texas, and that a Union expeditionary force under Maj. Gen. Nathaniel Banks was expected to invade that state in January. Semmes knew Galveston Harbor was shallow and that Union transports would have to anchor offshore. He hoped to swoop down with the *Alabama* and destroy a number of them. On the way to Galveston he hoped to intercept steamers from Panama. In those days before the Panama Canal, travelers to California went by steamer from New York to Aspinwall (now Colon) and then by rail across the Isthmus of Panama where they caught another steamer to San Francisco. Semmes hoped to catch at least one such ship traveling northward with gold.

Semmes took several ships before overhauling the large bark-rigged steamer *Ariel* of the Aspinwall Line on December 7. The

Alabama's most important prize, the *Ariel* was, unfortunately for Semmes, outward bound rather than returning from California with a rich cargo. She had on board more than 700 people, including some 500 passengers (half of them women and children) and a battalion of U.S. Marines (140 men) on their way to Pacific Squadron assignments. Semmes disarmed the marines and paroled them. He would have liked to have burned the ship but had no other vessel on which he could place her passengers. After several days he reluctantly let her go under bond. It was a big disappointment to Semmes that he could not burn her, especially as she was owned by Cornelius Vanderbilt, who had given the fast steamer *Vanderbilt* to the U.S. government for the express purpose of hunting down Confederate commerce raiders such as the *Alabama*.

Semmes then took the *Alabama* into the Gulf of Mexico and rendezvoused with the *Agrippina* at the Arcas Islands off the coast of Yucatán. There he prepared for his raid on Galveston. He planned to arrive during daylight, note Union dispositions, and return for a night attack when he could inflict the maximum damage and confusion. The plan appeared to have a good chance of success as the *Alabama* was faster than U.S. Navy blockaders along the coast and could run or fight on her choosing.

The *Alabama* arrived off Galveston in the late afternoon of the 11th. Semmes did not know that Galveston had been retaken ten days earlier and that the Banks expedition had been diverted to New Orleans. Instead of a fleet of Federal transports, the *Alabama*'s lookouts saw only five Union blockading warships lobbing shells into the Texas port city. Union seamen saw the *Alabama*, but they could not identify her. Suspicions were aroused, however, when Semmes stopped his ship some dozen miles offshore. The Union squadron commander, Commodore Henry H. Bell, flew his flag in the twenty-one-gun steam sloop *Brooklyn*, the same ship that had unsuccessfully chased the *Sumter* in her escape from New Orleans. Bell did not have his flagship available; she was immobilized by a nonfunctioning steam engine, so he sent the small, lightly armed *Hatteras*, under Lt. Commander Homer C. Blake, to investigate. A former Delaware River excursion side-wheel steamer, the *Hatteras* mounted only 4 x 32-pounders and a 20-pounder rifle.

Although the *Hatteras* was a poor match for the *Alabama*, this did not stop Semmes from later claiming the battle was an equal one. When the *Hatteras* put out, Semmes had the *Alabama* move slowly along the coast, drawing the Union warship away from the other blockaders. As soon as it was dark and when they were about twenty miles from the Federal squadron, the *Alabama* lay to and then turned toward the *Hatteras* under steam. The two ships were within hailing distance when Blake demanded his opponent's identity. Semmes identified his ship as a British steamer, whereupon Blake demanded the right to inspect the ship's registry in accordance with international law. After a boat had been lowered and was under way from the *Hatteras*, Lt. John M. Kell of the *Alabama* then called out, "This is the Confederate States steamer *Alabama*. Fire!"[7]

The battle took place at very short range, and both crews fired small arms as well as their main guns. The first broadside from the *Alabama* staggered the *Hatteras*. Knowing his ship's weakness, Blake tried to ram the *Alabama*, but the Confederate raider easily avoided him. The battle was over within thirteen minutes. With two of his men dead and five others wounded, his ship on fire and sinking, and the *Alabama* in position to rake, Blake surrendered. The *Alabama* had only two men wounded. Semmes took off the *Hatteras's* crew and speedily left the area. In late January he paroled his prisoners at Port Royal, Jamaica.

The *Alabama* remained in the West Indies for the next month, but on January 25, Semmes left Jamaica to sail east through the West Indies to Brazil. In the first three months of 1863 she took thirteen prizes. In April the cruiser arrived off Brazil to rendezvous with the *Agrippina*. In three months off Latin America, Semmes took fifteen more prizes. During this period he never spotted a U.S. Navy warship. U.S. Navy Adm. David Porter later penned a scathing assessment of efforts to intercept the Confederate raiders:

> It had never occurred to the American Government to send half-a-dozen gunboats or "double-enders" to these latitudes. They could have easily been spared, and a depot for coaling vessels could have been established under the smooth waters of the equator, at which all the vessels-of-war of the Navy could have been supplied. If the *Alabama* knew where to go to catch

American merchantmen, why did not the Federal Government know where to seek the *Alabama*? . . . It was not the particular smartness of Semmes that enabled him to escape capture. It was the omission or indifference of the Navy Department in not sending proper vessels to the right localities.[8]

With no sign of the *Agrippina*, which had been delayed and never linked up with the *Alabama*, Semmes recoaled from a prize and on April 22 took the *Alabama* back out to sea. Heading for Bahia, he captured several prizes en route and reached there on May 11. Two days later the CSS *Georgia* came in, and the CSS *Florida* was just one hundred miles to the north.

The only Union warship in the South Atlantic at the time was the screw sloop *Mohican*, sister ship to the *Kearsarge*. Acting Rear Admiral Wilkes, commander of the West Indian Squadron that was created specifically to track down the *Alabama* and *Florida*, had kept in the West Indies as his flagship the powerful fast steamer *Vanderbilt*, armed with 2 x 100-pounder rifled guns, 12 x 9-inch Dahlgren smoothbores, and 1 x 12-pounder rifle. She should have been operating with the *Mohican*, which missed the Confederate cruisers in several locations by only a few days. Wilkes, however, seemed more interested in capturing blockade runners for their prize money than in hunting the *Alabama*. Later, Secretary of the Navy Welles relieved him of command of the West Indian Squadron for "wholly inexcusable" misconduct in holding the *Vanderbilt*.

The *Alabama* took additional prizes, including on June 20 the 500-ton bark *Conrad*. A fine, fast clipper, she could be handled easily by a small crew. Semmes made her an auxiliary cruiser and commissioned her the *Tuscaloosa*, arming her with 2 x 12-pounders taken from one of the prizes. He made Lt. John Low her captain and transferred a dozen men as her crew. Semmes ordered the *Tuscaloosa* to proceed on her own and rendezvous with him at Cape Town, and Low subsequently captured two merchantmen. When the *Tuscaloosa* arrived at Cape Town, British authorities had to determine whether she was a legal warship. With London now pursuing a more strictly neutralist position, the British seized her in December 1863 as an uncondemned prize.

Semmes then sailed the *Alabama* to the Cape of Good Hope to intercept vessels homeward bound from the East Indies, arriving there at the end of July. In mid-August the *Alabama* was again cruising. In two months off South Africa she took only one prize. Semmes also learned of the Confederate defeats at Gettysburg, Vicksburg, and Port Hudson, and he discovered that the *Vanderbilt* was in the vicinity searching for him. The two ships played a game of cat-and-mouse for about a week. Time was running out for the *Alabama*. The year 1863 was the high point for Confederate commerce destroyers, and the *Alabama* took only three prizes in the first six months of 1864.

Semmes now took his ship into the Pacific. On September 24 the *Alabama* left Cape Town to sail through the Indian Ocean into the China Sea. To avoid the *Vanderbilt* he sailed far to the south of the island of Mauritius, but engine problems forced the *Vanderbilt* to give up the chase and return home. Semmes had hoped he could make serious inroads into U.S. merchantmen engaged in the Orient trade. In early November he took four merchantmen and burned them.

By now, however, Semmes was having trouble with his crew, who were dissatisfied with the lack of pay and liberty. Semmes also knew that the *Alabama* was wearing out. Her hull's copper plating was coming loose, and her boilers were so corroded that it was dangerous to use full steam.

On December 21 the *Alabama* arrived at Singapore. Rumors of the ship's presence had evidently preceded her, and Semmes found twenty-two U.S. merchant ships safely laid up in the harbor. Semmes heard of others secure at Bangkok, Canton, Shanghai, and Manila. At almost every port she touched, some men deserted; at Singapore twelve men left the ship but another six signed on.

From neutral ships, Semmes learned that the screw sloop *Wyoming*, a bark-rigged Federal gunboat (2 x 9-inch Dahlgrens in pivot and 4 x 32-pounders in broadsides) and the sole U.S. Navy warship on the China station, was patrolling Sunda Strait between Sumatra and Java. As the *Alabama* was somewhat more powerful, Semmes resolved to attack. Commander David M. McDougal of the *Wyoming* had learned of the presence of the *Alabama*. Believing she would continue into the China Sea, he sailed from Singapore for Manila, in the opposite direction as his adversary who had left Singapore on December 24.

The *Alabama* sailed through the Straits of Malacca taking some additional prizes and bringing the year's total to thirty-seven. By now crew morale was very low, the ship's bottom was very foul, and machinery was in poor repair. Semmes had already decided to seek a modern shipyard in Britain or France to carry out a complete overhaul of his vessel.

On December 31 the *Alabama* reentered the Indian Ocean. In the Bay of Bengal, she made a brief call at Anjenga on the southwestern Indian coast, where Semmes landed prisoners. She then sailed west to the Comoro Islands near the coast of Africa to reprovision and to let the crew have shore leave. On February 12 she left the Comoros, retracing her course back through the Indian Ocean to Cape Town, where she arrived on March 20. On the return trip, Semmes took only one vessel. At Cape Town, he learned that the British had seized the *Tuscaloosa*. He immediately lodged a protest, but the ship was eventually turned over to the American consul.

On March 25 the *Alabama* left Cape Town for Europe, where on the voyage via the Atlantic, she took her last two prizes, which Semmes ordered burned. The *Alabama*'s widely reported exploits were a considerable boost to Confederate morale, and Secretary Welles was determined that she be hunted down and destroyed. At one point or another twenty-five Union warships were engaged in searching for her, a considerable diversion of Union naval assets.

After nearly two years, most of which was spent at sea, the *Alabama* was worn out and badly in need of repairs. On June 11 the *Alabama* arrived at Cherbourg, France. Both Paris and London were well aware of the changing fortunes of the war in North America, and French officials pointed out that the dockyard was for French government ships only. Semmes believed that Emperor Napoléon III, who had sent a considerable military force to Mexico and thus had great interest in a Confederate victory, ultimately would grant approval.

While Semmes waited, news of the *Alabama*'s arrival reached the Dutch port of Flushing, where the Union third-rate steam screw sloop *Kearsarge*, commanded by Capt. John A. Winslow, was monitoring two other Confederate raiders, the *Georgia* and *Rappahannock*, at Calais. Winslow and his well-trained crew had spent a year searching for the *Alabama*. The *Kearsarge*, two months out of a Dutch dockyard and in excellent condition, was soon under way for Cherbourg. She arrived at Cherbourg on the 14th, and Winslow took up station to prevent the *Alabama* from escaping.

Although his ship was in poor condition, Semmes did not hesitate to do battle. It was partly a matter of pride; the war was about over, and there had been little glory in sinking merchantmen. But in fact he had little choice; delay would only bring more Union warships.

June 19 was a perfect day—partly hazy, with a calm sea and light wind from the west. A French ironclad, the *Couronne*, accompanied the *Alabama* as she left Cherbourg Harbor at about 9:30 A.M. The resulting battle off Cherbourg was one of the most spectacular Civil War naval engagements. Despite Semmes's later claims that the *Kearsarge* had the advantage, the two ships actually were closely matched. The *Kearsarge*'s 11 knots maximum speed made her slightly faster than her opponent. She had in broadside armament 4 x 32-pounder guns, mounted 1 x 30-pounder rifled gun, and had a small 12-pounder howitzer. Her strength, however, was in 2 x 11-inch pivot-mounted smoothbore Dahlgren guns that

An 11-inch Dahlgren after-pivot gun aboard USS *Kearsarge*. Naval Historical Center. NH 52025

threw 135-pound shells. Although the *Kearsarge* mounted seven guns, she could fight only five on one side. Her broadside weight of metal was about a quarter greater than that of her opponent (364 pounds to 274).

The *Alabama* also fought five guns on a side. Her armament consisted of eight guns: 6 x 32-pounders in broadside and two pivot-guns amidships (a 100-pounder rifled Blakeley and an 8-inch smoothbore). As the *Alabama* came out, Winslow had the *Kearsarge* steam off to the northeast, both to ensure that the battle would occur outside French territorial waters and to enable his ship to prevent the Confederate vessel from running back to the French shore. The *Alabama* followed. The *Couronne* took up position to mark the three-mile French territorial limit.

Semmes expected to use his starboard guns in broadside and shifted one 32-pounder from the port side to strengthen that battery. The added weight, however, caused the *Alabama* to list about two feet to starboard, which, however, was thought to be an advantage because it exposed less of that side of the vessel to enemy fire. When the two ships were about one and one quarter miles apart, Winslow reversed course and headed for the *Alabama*. He, too, planned to use his starboard battery, so the two ships met one another proceeding in opposite directions.

The battle began some six or seven miles offshore, and the entire action lasted a little longer than one hour. Just before 11:00, Semmes opened with a broadside at somewhat less than a mile. Several minutes later, at a range of about one-half mile, the *Kearsarge* replied. Winslow ordered a port turn to place his own ship in position to rake the *Alabama*. Semmes veered his ship to port to avoid this situation, but his maneuver allowed Winslow to close the range. As the *Alabama* turned back to starboard, the *Kearsarge* mirrored her movement. The *Kearsarge* was faster, and, as Winslow narrowed the range, the circles grew progressively smaller from one-half to one-quarter of a mile in diameter, with each ship firing her starboard batteries only. As they circled, the ships gradually drifted westwardly in the current.

The *Alabama* had the early advantage as her large Blakeley rifle had a longer range than any of her opponent's guns. The Federals were very lucky in that one Blakeley shell lodged in the *Kearsarge*'s wooden sternpost but failed to explode. Had it gone off, it would have destroyed her steering and made her unmanageable. Nonetheless, the *Kearsarge*'s steering became so difficult that it took four men to move the rudder.

The *Kearsarge* enjoyed an advantage in the cable chain strung over her vital middle parts to protect her engines, boilers, and magazines; this technique had been proven in fighting along the Mississippi River, and the chain had been in place for some time. In effect the Union warship was a partial ironclad. An outward sheathing of 1 inch of wood painted the same color as the rest of the hull concealed this from Confederate observation, but the French had informed Semmes about it.

The *Alabama* had chain in her lockers that might have been used for the same purpose. Later Semmes claimed he had been unaware of the *Kearsarge*'s chain mail, which he said was an unfair advantage. He seems to have convinced himself that this was the only reason that the *Alabama* lost the battle. Semmes could see through his spyglass that his shots that did strike were having no effect on the chain-protected side of the *Kearsarge*; they tore holes in the covering wood but did not pierce the chain beneath. Semmes then ordered the gun crews to fire higher. One shell tore through the *Kearsarge*'s smokestack; another sheared off the top of the engine-room hatch. Only one shot from the Confederate vessel caused personnel casualties aboard the Union ship: a shell that exploded on the quarterdeck wounded three men at the after-pivot gun, one mortally.

As the range narrowed, both sides substituted shell for solid shot. Semmes hoped to close on his opponent sufficiently to take the *Kearsarge* by boarding. Winslow refused to oblige and kept to a range that allowed his own guns to be most effective. Throughout, Winslow was able to dictate the range because his vessel was both faster and more maneuverable than the *Alabama*. Shell from the 11-inch Dahlgrens tore large holes in the latter's hull and had a terrible effect on her crew.

At the beginning of the eighth circle, when the two ships were about four hundred yards apart, Semmes realized that his ship was in sinking condition, and he turned her out of the circle in hopes of making the French shore. He also opened fire with his port battery, but the *Alabama* was taking on too much water and he was able to bring only two of her port guns to bear. The

Alabama was now completely at the mercy of the *Kearsarge*. With his vessel sinking, Semmes ordered all hands to abandon ship. Most of the *Alabama*'s boats had been destroyed or damaged in the battle, and most men simply leaped into the sea. The *Alabama* went down at 12:24 P.M.

Battle between the CSS *Alabama* and USS *Kearsarge*, June 19, 1864, off Cherbourg, France. Painting by Xanthus Smith, 1922. Naval Historical Center. K-29827

Perhaps surprisingly, the *Alabama* had gotten off many more shots in the battle—370—but less than 10 percent struck the *Kearsarge* (13 in and about the hull and 16 in the masts and rigging). These hits did little damage, and only three men aboard the *Kearsarge* were wounded, one of whom later died. Having incurred little damage, the *Kearsarge* was perfectly ready to fight again. Winslow reported that his ship had fired 173 shots and that a high percentage of these struck. One shot alone killed or wounded 18 men at the *Alabama*'s after-pivot gun. Shell fire from the heavy 11-inch pivot guns of the Union vessel had decided the engagement, especially a fortunate shot that damaged the *Alabama*'s steering apparatus. In all, there were 41 casualties aboard the Confederate vessel: 9 dead and 20 wounded in action and 12 men drowned.

The *Deerhound*, an English yacht that had been about a mile away during the battle, rescued forty-two Confederates, including Semmes, and took them all to Southampton, where they were released. Semmes later returned to the Confederacy, where he commanded the James River Squadron of three ironclad rams and seven wooden steamers for three months, until early April 1865, when Confederate forces abandoned Richmond and he had to destroy his ships.

The *Alabama*'s toll of sixty-six Union vessels taken nearly equaled the combined total of the two next most successful raiders: the *Shenandoah* with thirty-eight and the *Florida* with thirty-three. The sinking of the *Alabama* signaled the beginning of the end for Confederate commerce cruisers. By the summer of 1864 most of the raiders had been eliminated, and in October the *Florida* was taken. But the second most successful Confederate raider was commissioned late to the war and continued her depredations until well after the official end of hostilities.

Despite Confederate reverses on land, Mallory continued to press the war on the seas against Union commerce, and he instructed Bulloch in England to locate a vessel that might be quickly converted into a raider suitable for operations in the Pacific against the U.S. whaling fleet. By 1864 it was impossible for the Confederacy to build such a vessel in England because of tightened neutrality laws there, so it would have to be a conversion. Bulloch located such a vessel, purchasing her in September. She was the *Sea King*. One of the fastest screw steamships in the world, the *Sea King* had been built by Stevens & Son of Glasgow and launched only in August 1863; she had been designed for transporting troops to India. She weighed 1,160 tons and was 230' long, 32' in beam, and 20' 6" in depth of hold. Capable of 9 knots under steam, she had 1 screw, 2 boilers, and direct-acting engines. Flag Officer Samuel Barron, the ranking Confederate officer in Europe, named Lt. Commander James I. Waddell the *Sea King*'s captain and ordered him to destroy the Union whaling fleet in the Pacific.

On October 8 the *Sea King* slipped out of the Thames estuary, the last Confederate cruiser Bulloch got to sea. Under merchant captain G. H. Corbet, she appeared to be on a merchant voyage, but she proceeded to Funchal, Madeira, to rendezvous with the supply ship *Laurel*, which had sailed from England the same day with Waddell, the remainder of her crew, her armament, and stores. Her crew complement was seventy-three officers and men; and her armament consisted of 4 x 8-inch and 2 x 12-pounder smoothbore cannon and 2 x 32-pounder rifled guns. On October 19, 1864, Waddell officially commissioned the *Sea King* a Confederate warship under the name *Shenandoah* and began his cruise for Union vessels.

Waddell had hoped to secure the vast majority of the ship's original crew, but only twenty agreed to sign on. He obtained other volunteers en route, some of them from prizes. The *Shenandoah* took six Union prizes in the Atlantic. In mid-December she rounded the Cape of Good Hope, arriving at Melbourne, Australia, on January 25, 1865. There she underwent repairs. Without the dry docking and machinery repairs at Melbourne, Waddell would not have been able to undertake his subsequent mission; still, it was three weeks before repairs could be accomplished to the ship's propeller. Although a number of crewmen deserted at Melbourne, others took their place.

The *Shenandoah* sailed again on February 18 and cruised the whaling grounds in the Pacific Ocean and off Alaska. Her long stay at Melbourne had allowed U.S. whaling vessels in the South Pacific to be warned and disperse, but Waddell took the *Shenandoah* north and decimated the Union whaling fleet there. Reaching the Bering Sea on June 16, in six days, Waddell took twenty-four New England whaling vessels, burning all but those necessary to ship his prisoners. Threading through dangerous ice floes, the *Shenandoah* managed to escape being trapped and crushed.

One of his captives told Waddell that the war was over, but there was no newspaper clipping or piece of evidence, and for some time, Waddell refused to believe it. Later he secured newspapers that reported that the Confederate government had moved from Richmond and that President Davis had proclaimed that the war would continue. Fortified with this information, Waddell took nineteen additional prizes in four days, sparing only those necessary for his prisoners. The *Shenandoah* then headed south along the coast. Waddell hoped to carry out a daring night raid into San Francisco Bay to seize the Union monitor *Comanche* and exact a ransom from the city.

Finally, on August 2, 1865, Waddell accepted a report from an English captain as proof of the end of the war. Waddell struck the ship's guns below and sailed the *Shenandoah* seventeen thousand miles without stopping to Liverpool, England. Arriving there on November 6, he surrendered to British authorities.

The trip had been made virtually under sail alone. Waddell resorted to steam only once, at night in the mid-South Atlantic to elude the USS *Saranac*. In the process, the *Shenandoah* became the only Confederate warship to sail around the world. In all, the *Shenandoah* took thirty-eight Union vessels, of which Waddell burned thirty-two. The remainder he had sent under cartel, with the prisoners, to San Francisco. Damage to Union shipping was estimated at $1.36 million. In 1866 the *Shenandoah* was sold to the Sultan of Zanzibar, and she sank in the Indian Ocean in September 1872.

During the Civil War the Confederate commerce raiders destroyed some 257 U.S. merchant ships, or about 5 percent of the total. They drove up insurance rates substantially, but they hardly disrupted U.S. trade nor did they disturb the Union blockade, which became steadily more effective as the war progressed. Cruisers employed by the U.S. Navy to hunt down the Confederate raiders cost the government approximately $3,325,000. During 14 months from January 1863, a total of 72 warships and 23 chartered vessels were used in this effort.

The main effect of the commerce raiders was to force a substantial number of U.S. vessels into permanent foreign registry. During the 4 years of war, more than 700 U.S. ships transferred to British registry alone. Historian George Dalzell stated that the *Alabama* and other Confederate cruisers inflicted great long-range damage on the U.S. merchant marine in causing the flight of so many U.S. vessels to foreign registry. He concluded that more than half the total U.S. merchant fleet was permanently lost to the flag during the Civil War. The cruisers burned or sank 110,000 tons, but another 800,000 tons were sold to foreign owners—and these were the best ships. The ones left were those that the foreigners did not want. Legal impediments prevented this tonnage from returning.

After the war, that the British government had allowed the fitting out of a number of the Confederate cruisers became a major stumbling block in Anglo-American relations. Washington believed, rightly or wrongly, that London's early proclamation of neutrality and then persistent disregard of it in the early period of the war had heartened the South and prolonged the conflict. There were those in the U.S. government who proposed taking British Western Hemisphere possessions, including Canada, as compensation.

In January 1871, when the European balance of power decisively changed with Prussia's defeat of France, British statesmen concluded that it might be wise to reach some accommodation with the United States against the possibility of a German drive for world hegemony. An international tribunal met in Geneva in December 1871 over what became known as the "*Alabama* claims," and in September 1872, it awarded the U.S. government $15,500,500 in damages. This settlement has come to be regarded as an important step forward in the peaceful settlement of international disputes and a victory for the world rule of law.

NOTES

1. William M. Robinson, Jr., *The Confederate Privateers* (1928; reprint ed., Columbia: University of South Carolina Press, 1980), 342.

2. Porter, *Naval History of the Civil War*, 602.

3. Ibid., 605.

4. Ibid., 605–6.

5. *ORN*, series 1, vol. 1 (Washington, DC: Government Printing Office, 1894), 766–67.

6. Ibid.

7. Raphael Semmes, *Memoirs of Service Afloat during the War between the States* (1869; reprint, Secaucus, NJ: Blue and Grey Press, 1987), 543.

8. Porter, *Naval History of the Civil War*, 642.

CHAPTER SIX

UNION COASTAL OPERATIONS

FOLLOWING HIS FAILURE at Vicksburg in mid-1862, Admiral Farragut devoted his attention to closing off the Texas coast. He ordered the establishment of Union bases ashore there, thus doubling the advantage of closing the coast to blockade runners and providing bases for the Union ships. By mid-October 1862, Farragut had secured Pensacola, through its evacuation by the Confederates, as well as Corpus Christi, Sabine Pass, and Port Lavaca, and the major Texas seaport of Galveston.

GALVESTON

The Federals had begun a blockade of Galveston in July 1861, but it was not until October 4, 1862, that Union forces actually attempted to take the city. On that date Commander William B. Renshaw moved his squadron, which included the *Westfield* (flagship), *Harriet Lane*, *Owasco*, *Clifton*, and mortar schooner *Henry James*, into the harbor and demanded that the city surrender. The Confederate commander ashore, Col. Joseph J. Cook, agreed, but only on condition of a four-day truce, during which he supervised the removal of Galveston's guns, military equipment, and personnel.

To assist in the occupation of Galveston, the little gunboats *Corypheus* and *Sachem* arrived from New Orleans, along with three companies of troops of the 54th Massachusetts Infantry. The troops took up position along the waterfront so that they might be supported by the Union squadron in the event of a Confederate land attack.

Confederate Maj. Gen. John B. Magruder, who assumed command of military forces in Texas at the end of November, made retaking Galveston a priority. To accomplish this goal and to break the Union blockade, he planned a joint army-navy operation. While Confederate land forces assaulted the Union troops, a naval force would prevent the Union ships close to shore from providing assistance. Magruder launched his attack on January 1 before dawn.

Confederate Maj. Leon Smith commanded a little squadron of makeshift warships. Smith's men had placed artillery on them, protecting their guns and themselves with bales of cotton. The flotilla included "cottonclads" *Bayou City* and *Neptune*, which also carried some one hundred army sharpshooters and boarders each. Armed tenders *John F. Carr* and *Lucy Gwin* accompanied them.

Commander Renshaw had seven ships in his squadron. Unfortunately for the Union side, at the beginning of the attack, when Renshaw moved the *Westfield* to assist the troops ashore, his ship grounded in Bolivar Channel. It could not be gotten off during the subsequent battle, despite assistance from the *Clifton*.

Although the Union squadron had been caught off guard, its men put up a strong fight, particularly the *Harriet Lane* under Commander Jonathan M. Wainwright. He ordered his ship to ram the *Bayou City*, which, although accomplished, did not cause much damage. The iron-hulled *Harriet Lane* was in turn rammed by the *Neptune*, which was so damaged in the impact that shot from the *Harriet Lane* at her waterline caused her to sink. Fortunately for the Confederates aboard, the water was only eight feet deep. The *Bayou City*, meanwhile, turned and rammed the *Harriet Lane*. The force of the collision so entangled the two ships that they could not be separated. Confederate troops aboard the *Bayou City* rushed aboard the *Harriet Lane*, taking her by storm. Commander Wainwright and his executive officer were among Union defenders killed.

The Confederates arranged a truce and offered Renshaw the opportunity to take his men and depart in one of his ships if he surrendered. Renshaw, determined to prevent the capture of his ship, refused. He ordered Lt. Commander Richard L. Law, captain of the *Clifton*, to withdraw the remaining Union vessels from the harbor and escape while he scuttled the *Westfield*. With his ship soon in flames, Renshaw and his boat crew were killed when fire reached the magazine before they could get clear. Law did succeed, under a hail of Confederate fire, in removing the remaining Union vessels to safety.

The daring Confederate attack had recaptured Galveston and reopened the port to blockade runners. The Confederates also had destroyed two Union warships and killed or captured 414 Union soldiers and seamen. The cost to their own side was modest: 1 ship lost and personnel casualties of 26 dead and 117 wounded. Galveston remained in Confederate hands for the remainder of the war.

Farragut moved immediately to reestablish the blockade off Galveston, but on January 11, as noted in Chapter 5, the *Alabama* unexpectedly arrived and sank the *Hatteras*, a further blow to Union pride. Then, on January 21 at Sabine Pass, the blockade was again broken by the cotton-clad steamers *Uncle Ben* and *Bell*. Armed with artillery and infantry, they attacked Union blockading sailing vessels *Morning Light* and *Velocity*. The Union warships were handicapped by the absence of any appreciable wind. Taking up a raking position at close range, the Confederates riddled the *Morning Light* and forced her to surrender. The *Velocity* then was also struck by fire.

Texas assumed increasing importance to the Union war effort, thanks to the French military presence in Mexico. France, Britain, and Spain had occupied Vera Cruz, Mexico's City's chief port, to secure debts owed their nationals. Emperor Napoléon III planned to stay, and, after the British and Spanish troops departed, French troops campaigned to the interior. In June 1863 they took Mexico City. Fears mounted in Washington (not without reason) that the French planned to resurrect the Republic of Texas.

A major Union expedition was then organized to take Sabine Pass. Consisting of four thousand ground troops in transports, the expedition was convoyed by the gunboats *Clifton*, *Sachem*, *Arizona*, and *Granite City*. The *Clifton* (2 x 9-inch and 4 x 32-pounders) was the largest Union warship, and all were of shallow draft so that they could enter the river. But these warships, with their light armament, were no match for the Confederate guns ashore, and the Union attack on September 8, 1863, was repulsed. Both the *Clifton* and *Sachem* had their boilers ruptured and were surrendered, suffering a combined loss of sixty-five men. The expedition was then abandoned.

Union forces had better luck at Brazos Island, near the mouth of the Rio Grande. It was taken on November 2 by a Union force of 2,500 men, supported by a squadron under her captain, Commander James H. Strong, consisting of the *Monongahela* (flagship), *Owasco*, and *Virginia*. Union forces subsequently took Brownsville and Corpus Christi, Texas. An effort against Galveston was abandoned for lack of resources. With an expedition in the offing up the Red River to take Texas from the east rather than the southwest, the Union troops in the Galveston area were withdrawn.

Union forces also mounted joint operations in the east. On January 7–9, 1863, Commodore Foxhall A. Parker led another Union army-navy operation, this one up the Pamunkey River, a tributary of the York in Virginia. *Mahaska* and *Commodore Morris* supported the army movement and convoyed the transport *May Queen* up the Pamunkey in the joint effort. Before withdrawing because of low water and obstructions, Foxhall destroyed a number of Confederate boats, barges, and stores at West Point and White Horse. This relatively modest operation was typical of a great number of such efforts mounted by the U.S. Navy during the war. Using its control of the sea, the navy was able to keep the Confederates off guard, force them to disperse forces, and destroy stocks of war matériel.

BATTLE OF MOBILE BAY

In 1864 the war entered its third year. In the east, Richmond stood defiant, while in the west, most of the Confederate heartland lay unconquered. Death tolls were mounting, and war weariness had spread on both sides as the conflict threatened to continue indefinitely. Indeed, Lincoln's reelection even appeared in jeopardy. To oppose him the Democrats nominated Gen. George B. McClellan. They also adopted a peace plank calling for immediate cessation of hostilities and the restoration of peace "on the basis of the Federated Union of the States." Although McClellan repudiated that position, he clearly sought to capitalize on the war weariness. Were McClellan to win the election, most people assumed that the war would be brought to a negotiated end.

Lincoln's new general-in-chief since March, Lt. Gen. Ulysses S. Grant, was all too aware of this situation, and in the spring of 1864 he developed a plan to smash Confederate resistance in both the eastern and western theaters and secure Lincoln's reelection. Simultaneous offensives were to begin in May. The eastern strategy relied on superior Union numbers. Its centerpiece was a massive thrust southward by the Army of the Potomac against Richmond, supported by secondary operations up the James, up the Shenandoah Valley, and from West Virginia. These advances were to present Gen. Robert E. Lee with a multiplicity of fronts and prevent reinforcement of his Army of Northern Virginia, which was facing the Army of the Potomac driving on Richmond.

In the west, Grant's plan called for the destruction of Gen. Joseph E. Johnston's Army of Tennessee by a two-pronged effort. Utilizing the key railhead of Chattanooga, Tennessee, Maj. Gen. William T. Sherman would drive into Georgia. At the same time a Union naval force would secure Mobile Bay, allowing another Union army to drive north from Mobile, Alabama. This land force would divert Southern resources south of Sherman.

Mobile Bay and its port of Mobile were vital to the Southern war effort. After the Tredegar Iron Works in Richmond, Alabama was the second Southern center for manufacturing iron and rolling heavy iron plate. The Confederacy also had established at Selma a second facility capable of producing the heaviest guns. Mobile also was one of the few deep-water ports then available to the Confederacy, and the city itself, thirty miles from the Gulf of Mexico, was an important transshipment point by blockade runners for goods that could be sent upriver from there to the interior.

Farragut had wanted to proceed against Mobile after taking New Orleans in the spring of 1862, but he had been obliged to operate on the Mississippi, principally against Vicksburg, in the Union effort to open the river. The resulting delay allowed the Confederates time to strengthen Mobile's defenses. After he had taken Vicksburg, General Grant also favored a move against Mobile, but Lincoln and Maj. Gen. Henry Halleck, then Union general-in-chief, had other priorities. When Grant took over direction of all Union armies and Halleck became his chief of staff, Grant was in a position to dictate strategy.

Grant was disappointed that an early effort against Mobile had to be put off. Major General Banks already had demonstrated his incompetence trying to open the lower Mississippi River in operations against Port Hudson after the Union capture of Vicksburg in 1863. Now Banks's thirty thousand-man army, scheduled to operate against Mobile in May, was roughly handled in the Red River Campaign to occupy northwestern Louisiana.

Grant focused on Mobile as his next target in the west, but before that campaign could be launched, President Lincoln authorized an expedition against Shreveport, Louisiana, headquarters for Lieut. Gen. Kirby Smith and a major supply depot and gateway to Texas. The resulting March to May 1864 Red River Campaign was a minor disaster for Union forces.

After that fiasco, Lincoln accepted the inevitable and Banks was removed from command. His replacement, Maj. Gen. E. R. S. Canby, was an able professional officer. On his way to his New Orleans headquarters, Canby received a telegram from Sherman on June 4 requesting that he carry out a strong feint or real attack against Mobile. Sherman had a sizable numerical advantage and was then closing in on Atlanta. But the Confederate force defending against his approach remained basically intact, and Sherman wanted to make certain that it was not reinforced. He urged Canby to attack from Pascagoula, Mississippi, in cooperation with naval units under Admiral Farragut.

Two weeks later, on June 17, Canby met with Farragut aboard the *Hartford* with the Union blockading ships off Mobile Bay to plan the attack. They decided to reduce Confederate Forts Morgan and Gaines, guarding the entrance to Mobile Bay, by joint army-navy assault. After that attack, a land force would advance on Mobile from Pascagoula. The navy would take care of Fort Powell, an earthen fortification in Mississippi Sound. Canby anticipated no problem in securing the twenty thousand land troops required. Farragut, however, was concerned about obtaining ironclads, which he deemed essential.

In March 1864, Confederate Brig. Gen. Richard L. Page, who had served in the U.S. Navy for 37 years prior to the Civil War, assumed command of the outer defenses of Mobile Bay. Under his supervision the Confederates constructed or reinforced forts to cover the channel leading into the bay and the approaches to

Mobile itself. Fort Morgan was the principal bastion. An old casemated masonry structure begun in 1818, it was located at the tip of Mobile Point, a long neck of land that jutted out and controlled the entrance to the bay. Fort Morgan mounted 45 guns. Two other forts were located up the channel: Fort Gaines on the eastern tip of Dauphin Island and, further along, Fort Powell at Cedar Point. The defenders had implanted pilings as obstructions in the channel between Forts Morgan and Gaines and on both sides of Fort Powell. Between the pilings and Fort Morgan the channel was further narrowed by 180 submerged torpedoes. Fitted with percussion caps or fulminate of mercury fuses, they were rigged to explode their main charges when struck by a passing vessel. The torpedoes were ranged in 3 parallel rows. Most had been in the water for some time, however, and a number were defective. Only a few new ones had been deployed. The remaining channel for shipping from the beach to a marker buoy was quite narrow, only about 150 to 200 yards wide.

In the bay itself, Confederate Adm. Franklin Buchanan commanded a small squadron. In August 1862, after his recovery from the wound that he had received aboard the *Virginia*, Buchanan was promoted to rear admiral, and Mallory assigned him to Mobile. Buchanan pinned his hopes on the ironclad ram *Tennessee II*, by far his most powerful vessel. Supporting her were three small gunboats: the *Gaines*, *Selma*, and *Morgan*.

The 3 gunboats were of little consequence. The *Gaines* and *Morgan* were of similar class. Built in 1862 they were 863-ton side-wheelers, 202' x 38' x 7' 3" in size and armed with 1 x 7-inch and 1 x 6-inch rifled gun, 2 x 32-pounder rifled guns, and 1 x 32-pounder smoothbore. The *Selma*, only 320 tons, was 252' x 30' x 6'. A converted coastal packet and also a side-wheeler, she was built in 1856 and acquired by the Confederacy in April 1861. She mounted 3 rifled guns, 1 x 9-inch, 1 x 8-inch, and 1 x 6-inch.

The ironclad *Tennessee II* (usually referred to simply as the *Tennessee*) was another matter. One of the most powerful of Confederate ironclad rams of the war, she was laid down at Selma, some 150 miles upriver from Mobile, in October 1862. Launched in February 1863, she was commissioned in February 1864. She was 209' overall (189' between perpendiculars) x 48' x 14'. A modified *Columbia*-class (*Columbia* and *Texas*) ironclad, she had their distinctive shorter casemate, 79' long. Heavily armored, she had 6 inches of iron on her casemate, 5 inches on her sides, and 2 inches on deck. She mounted 6 Brooke rifles: 2 x 7-inch on pivot mounts fore and aft and 4 x 6.4-inch in broadsides. Inadequately powered for her weight, however, she was difficult to maneuver. Her principal defect, as it turned out, was her relatively exposed rudder chains that ran in channels in her afterdeck.

Despite these defenses, Farragut planned to repeat his successes on the Mississippi by running past the forts, quickly destroying the Confederate squadron in the bay, then returning to pound the forts into submission. Maj. Gen. Gordon Granger's IV Corps would then land and assist in taking the forts.

The CSS *Tennessee. ORN,* series 1, vol. 21(Washington, DC: Government Printing Office, 1906), frontispiece.

Initially, Farragut had only fourteen warships in his squadron: five big screw sloops—the *Brooklyn, Hartford, Richmond, Lackawanna,* and *Monongahela;* three smaller screw sloops—the *Ossipee, Oneida,* and *Seminole;* two screw gunboats, the *Kennebec* and *Itasca;* three side-wheel gunboats, the *Octorara, Metacomet,* and *Port Royal;* and only one ironclad, the rather unsatisfactory *Galena.* To have any chance of success, he would need more ironclads. He requested that the Navy Department provide as many as possible, and Secretary Welles complied.

In the east, Grant accompanied his major field army, the Army of the Potomac, as it pushed south toward Richmond. Lee parried Grant's blows and inflicted casualties equivalent to the size of his own force, but his own Army of Northern Virginia never recovered from Grant's relentless attacks. Grant then sought to maneuver in behind Lee at Petersburg, south of Richmond, but Lee was too quick for him. The two sides then settled down to a long siege, a harbinger of World War I trench warfare.

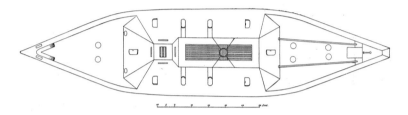

The CSS *Tennessee* deck plan. *ORN*, series 1, vol. 21 (Washington, DC: Government Printing Office, 1906), 582.

Operations in the east affected preparations in the west. On July 1, Canby received a dispatch from General Halleck in Washington requesting that he detach as many troops as he could spare and send them to Fortress Monroe. With Lee's Army of Northern Virginia under siege at Petersburg, Grant wanted to increase his force sharply there to avoid a protracted siege. Canby informed Farragut that the attack on Mobile had been canceled.

Farragut was not pleased with this development. However, he was somewhat mollified that Canby was working to revive the operation and was relieved to learn that the ironclad *Manhattan* had arrived at Pensacola. Then, only a week after the attack had been canceled, Canby told Farragut that he could make available four thousand men to operate against the two Confederate forts. Although this force would not be sufficient to take Mobile, it would enable Farragut to go ahead with his plan to force the entrance to, and secure, Mobile Bay. Farragut immediately plunged ahead with planning. On July 12 he issued General Order No. 10, which directed crews of the squadron to remove any unnecessary spars and rigging from their vessels and to protect valuable machinery with sandbags and chains.

Six days later Canby informed Farragut that there would be a "delay" in putting together the troops to assault the forts. Farragut replied that time was running out and that favorable weather would not hold much longer. He was willing, he said, to proceed if the army could provide as few as one thousand men to attack Fort Gaines. They could then continue on to Fort Morgan after Gaines had surrendered. The arrival of the *Manhattan* from Pensacola, along with word that two other monitors also would arrive shortly, emboldened Farragut.

On the 26th, Canby informed Farragut that he had put together two thousand men for the operation against Fort Gaines. Another three thousand men would shortly be available after the evacuation of Union garrisons in Texas, and they would be sent on as reinforcements. Three days later, on the 19th, Canby told Farragut that he was embarking twenty-four hundred men for Dauphin Island.

Farragut then issued General Order No. 11 for the operation. All the vessels were to pass to the east of the easternmost buoy in the area clear of obstructions. Any disabled vessels were to drop out of the line to westward and make no further attempt to enter the bay until all the rest of the squadron had passed. Once the Union ships had entered the bay, the smaller gunboats would try to prevent the Confederate gunboats from escaping up the bay.

Farragut was concerned not only about the obstacles but also about torpedoes. Refugees and deserters had reported that many of them were watersoaked and probably unreliable, but they did not know locations or numbers and could provide no other information on the underwater obstacles. On several occasions, Farragut had his flag lieutenant, John C. Watson, conduct night reconnaissances, but, given the circumstances, Watson was unable to discover anything.

On July 31 the double-turreted monitor *Winnebago* arrived at Sand Island and anchored near the *Manhattan*. She brought the welcome news that the *Chickasaw* was close behind. Farragut then sent Capt. Thornton Jenkins in the *Richmond* to Pensacola to hurry along the *Tecumseh*. Farragut's flag captain, Percival Drayton, told Jenkins to stay in Pensacola until the *Tecumseh* was ready. On

August 1, General Granger met with Farragut aboard the latter's flagship and informed him that army troops would land on the west end of Dauphin Island to work their way toward Fort Gaines at the other end.

The double-turreted *Chickasaw* then arrived from New Orleans. With the *Tecumseh* expected momentarily, Farragut had the force he thought he needed. The four monitors—single-turreted *Manhattan* and *Tecumseh*, each with 2 x 15-inch Dahlgrens, and double-turreted *Chickasaw* and *Winnebago*, armed with 4 x 11-inch Dahlgren smoothbores—brought his squadron up to eighteen warships. Farragut set the date for the attempt at August 4.

On August 3, as Granger's transports steamed up Mississippi Sound toward Dauphin Island, Farragut met with his captains aboard the *Hartford*. He had wanted his own ship to lead, but his captains persuaded him that she was too exposed. Farragut reluctantly agreed that this honor would go to the *Brooklyn*, commanded by Capt. James Alden and equipped with four bow chaser guns and a torpedo catcher. Farragut would have cause to regret this decision.

Later, on the afternoon of the 3d, Farragut learned that the *Tecumseh* would not arrive in time. Unhappy, he informed Jenkins, still in Pensacola, that the army troops were about to go ashore and that he was to return to the squadron on the 4th, with or without the *Tecumseh*. Farragut would wait no longer: "I can lose no more days," he commented.[1] Still later that afternoon some fifteen hundred Union troops landed unopposed on the west end of Dauphin Island. The next day, Union and Confederate troops could be heard firing at one another on the island. Embarrassed about the failure of his squadron to attack on schedule, especially with Confederate vessels landing men and supplies at Fort Gaines, Farragut ordered his double-turreted monitor *Winnebago* to drive them off. The ironclad got to about one thousand yards of the fort and lobbed twenty-four shots in its direction; Fort Gaines responded with several shots of its own. Little was accomplished on either side.

Farragut met aboard the *Hartford* for a final time with his captains later on the 4th and went over his instructions. The monitors *Tecumseh* (if she arrived in time), *Manhattan*, *Winnebago*, and *Chickasaw* would be closest to Fort Morgan, to the right of another column of his larger wooden screw sloops consisting, in order, of the *Brooklyn, Hartford, Richmond, Lackawanna, Mononga-hela, Ossipee,* and *Oneida.* The ironclads would help mask the wooden vessels from the heavy guns of Fort Morgan. Quantities of heavy chain draped over their unprotected sides served as makeshift armor for the wooden ships. Farragut also employed a tactic similar to that used against Port Hudson; he ordered the seven smallest wooden ships, four side-wheel gunboats, two screw gunboats, and a screw steamer lashed to the port sides of the larger wooden screw steamers to provide additional layers of protection. These were, in order, the *Octorara, Metacomet, Port Royal, Seminole, Kennebec, Itasca,* and *Galena.*

Farragut ordered the ships to approach in echelon to starboard to provide their bow guns a free field of fire. He planned to take his squadron as close as possible to Fort Morgan, believing that broadsides fire would be his ships' best defense. They would proceed at low steam. At the same time, Farragut would have supporting vessels lay down suppressive fire on the forts. Lt. Commander E. C. Grafton's Gulf Flotilla of six gunboats would shell Fort Morgan from the Gulf, while Lt. Commander J. C. P. De Kraft's Mississippi Sound Flotilla of five small gunboats shelled Fort Powell.

At about 4:30 P.M. the *Richmond* returned from Pensacola, bringing with her the *Tecumseh* under tow by the side-wheeler *Bienville.* At dusk the ships that would make the run into the bay steamed beyond the bar and anchored in line abreast on either side of the *Brooklyn.*

At 3:00 on the morning of August 5, 1864, all hands were called to stations. Final preparations were made and sandwiches distributed. A proper breakfast would be served after the battle. The ships formed up in pairs, and at 5:30 the *Hartford* hoisted the signal "Get Underway." Farragut's eighteen ships, including the four ironclad monitors, steamed into the bay. The monitors had key roles to play. The *Tecumseh* and *Manhattan* were to engage the *Tennessee* and keep her away from the more vulnerable wooden warships, while the *Winnebago* and *Chickasaw* were charged with laying down suppressive fire against the Fort Morgan.

Shortly after 6:00 A.M. the first Union ships crossed the bar. About this time the morning mist cleared, and from every peak,

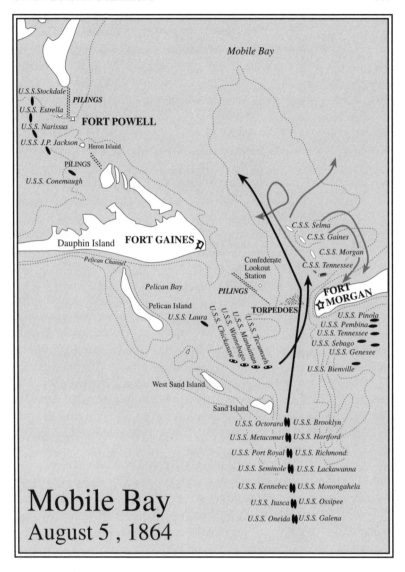

Mobile Bay
August 5 , 1864

staff, and masthead hung a large U.S. flag. Conditions were ideal for the Union side. A light southwest breeze would inhibit vision for the Confederates by blowing smoke away from the Union ships and toward the forts. A flood tide helped compensate for the low steam ordered aboard the Union ships. The Confederates, however, would have the advantage of being able to rake the Union ships with their fire during the approach.

When Flag Officer Buchanan was informed that Union ships had begun crossing the bar, he ordered the captain of the *Tennessee*, Commander James D. Johnston, to get under way. In short order, Buchanan had placed his little squadron in line-ahead formation across the channel and adjacent to the torpedo field. The smaller vessels were to the west of the flagship. Buchanan hoped to "cross the T" of the Union line and in this way be able to rake the advancing Union ships with some sixteen guns, most of them long-range rifles. As Buchanan addressed the crew of the *Tennessee*, exhorting them to continue the fight and in no case to surrender, troops at Fort Morgan were manning their eighteen guns, ready to add their fire to that of Buchanan's ships.

The *Tecumseh* led the Union column and was well out in front of the other ships. Her captain, Commander Tunis A. M. Craven, was unfamiliar with the bay and its shoals, but he had aboard a pilot, John Collins, who knew the bay and its waters very well. Collins did not, however, know anything about the characteristics of the ironclad. Her guns were loaded with shell; as soon as they were fired, they would be recharged with solid shot for the *Tennessee*. At about 6:47 the *Tecumseh* opened fire, but General Page thought the range too great and would not authorize return fire from the fort. He would not do so until 7:05, with the *Tecumseh* still some two thousand yards distant and the rest of the squadron nearly three thousand yards. The *Brooklyn* then returned fire and the engagement became general. One of the most important, and certainly the bloodiest, naval battles of the Civil War had begun.

Commander Craven, peering through the narrow slits of the *Tecumseh*'s pilothouse, could see the *Tennessee* six hundred yards ahead. The *Manhattan* followed in the *Tecumseh*'s wake, but the *Brooklyn* was gaining on the port quarter. The ironclads were to engage the *Tennessee* and keep her away from the wooden ships, but the *Brooklyn* now threatened to overtake the monitors and enter the bay first.

Alden on the *Brooklyn* realized that a serious situation was developing. He could not afford to be in advance of the two leading ironclads, and the *Chickasaw* and *Winnebago* were too far west of Fort Morgan to allow the wooden vessels to pass east of the

minefield. The *Tennessee* lay in wait on the other side of the torpedoes, and Buchanan was ready to ram the first Union ship to
emerge into the bay. He hoped that by sinking a large Union ship
in the narrow channel between Fort Morgan and the torpedo field,
he might deny the others access to the bay and force them to retire back into the Gulf.

Alden ordered one of the army flagmen brought aboard the
squadron for the operation to signal the flagship: "The Monitors
are right ahead. We cannot go on without passing them. What
shall we do?"[2] It was difficult to get answers back and forth
through the smoke. Lt. John Kinney had to climb one hundred
feet above the deck into the *Hartford*'s crosstrees to see the *Brooklyn* over the smoke and send the reply, "Go ahead." By the time
this message reached Alden, the *Brooklyn* already had overtaken
two of the monitors and was abreast of the *Manhattan*.[3] The *Hartford* and *Richmond* also were closing fast. The other Union ships,
their captains seeing the confusion ahead, fell behind.

Craven on the *Tecumseh* doubted that he could pass to the
east of the red buoy and change course in time to engage the *Tennessee* before she could ram the Union wooden ships. The Confederate ironclad, some two hundred yards ahead, had actually
moved a bit to the west to be in a better position for precisely the
maneuver Craven feared. This situation prompted Craven to order his ironclad to skirt inside the line of Confederate mines and
make directly for the *Tennessee* to engage her at once.

As the distance between the two ironclads closed, suddenly
there was a terrific explosion. The *Tecumseh* had struck a mine.
She rolled to port, her bow down and her stern lifted up, her
screw propeller turning madly in the air. The *Tecumseh* sank
quickly, disappearing within four minutes. Craven and pilot
Collins left the pilothouse and met at the foot of the ladder to the
escape hatch on the turret, struggling in water already up to their
chests. "After you, pilot," Craven said. It was the last words he
uttered, for Collins was the twenty-first and last man free of the
ship. He recalled, "There was nothing after me, for when I reached
the top rung of the ladder the vessel seemed to drop from under
me."[4]

Ninety-three officers and men, including Craven, perished
aboard the *Tecumseh*. Some of the survivors made it into one of

the ironclad's boats that had somehow floated free. Others were picked up by a cutter from one of the sloops, and four men swam to shore where they were made prisoners. Both sides were so stunned by the explosion that fire slackened for a few moments before it resumed.

The *Brooklyn* signaled back to the *Hartford*, "Our best monitor has been sunk." Lieutenant Kinney, still in the crosstrees, relayed the message to Farragut. Within minutes, Kinney signaled Farragut's instructions back to Alden that the monitors were to proceed and the *Brooklyn* was to take her place in the line. The *Hartford* was now dangerously close to the *Brooklyn*, and the *Richmond* was not far behind the flagship.

The *Brooklyn* in effect now blocked the channel. Farragut, lashed in the mizzen shrouds of the *Hartford* to be able to see the battle unfolding over the thick smoke, could see the Union ships behind him slow to a near halt and bunch up. General Page at Fort Morgan ordered his gun crews to fire as fast as they could at the now stationary Union ships; casualties aboard the ships mounted as Confederate shells from the fort found their mark. Had it not been for Farragut's orders that the Union fleet run close to the fort and keep up a steady fire of grape and shrapnel against it, the Union ships would have been even worse off.

It appeared that the Confederates might win the battle. Clearly this moment was the decisive point, and Farragut knew it. When Alden failed to advance, despite three orders from Farragut to go ahead, the admiral took action himself. He knew that if he could get a sufficient number of his ships into the bay, he could close it to blockade runners forever.

There was a major risk from other mines, and Farragut chose to take that chance with his own ship. He got the attention of his pilot, Martin Freeman, and asked if there was sufficient depth of water for the *Hartford* to pass on the port side of the *Brooklyn*. Freemen said that there was but asked about the torpedoes. Farragut then told Freeman to pick his way into the bay or blow up.

The *Hartford* got up speed and passed on the port side of the *Brooklyn*. As she overtook the leading Union ship, Farragut shouted, "What's the trouble?" "Torpedoes," was the reply.

"Damn the torpedoes," Farragut said. He then ordered his ship to get up speed, and, finally, he called to the captain of the gunboat lashed to the side of the *Hartford*, "Go ahead, Jouett, full speed!" Farragut's words have passed into history in shortened version as, "Damn the torpedoes; full speed ahead!"[5]

Fortunately for Farragut and the men of the Union squadron, many of the primer tubes and fuses in the torpedoes were corroded from long immersion in the salt water. As the *Hartford* pushed past the *Brooklyn* and into the minefield, men below decks on the *Hartford* could hear primers going off and mines bumping into the hull beneath them, but none of them exploded. By 7:50 the *Hartford* was clear of the minefield and into the bay.

Although the Union ships fired into Fort Morgan as they passed it, the fort gave better than it took, and the last ships in the Union line sustained considerable damage. The *Oneida* was the principal casualty. Her boiler knocked out and rudder cables cut, she was dead in the water, but her consort, the *Galena*, managed to tow her to safety.

Buchanan, aboard the *Tennessee*, saw Farragut's pennant on the *Hartford* and ordered the ironclad to make for her. The Confederate gunboats joined in, raking the Union flagship. Buchanan's effort to ram was unsuccessful; the *Tennessee* did not have sufficient speed, and the more nimble *Hartford* was easily able to avoid her lunge. The ram passed by the Union flagship, both vessels firing at one another. Buchanan then gave up on the flagship, seeking to engage the sloops that were following.

As the *Hartford* steamed up the channel, the smaller Confederate gunboats maintained position on her starboard bow, firing into her at close range with devastating effect. Soon, however, the Union flagship brought her own guns to bear and drove them off. Farragut ordered the *Metacomet* and other smaller vessels cut free to attack the other Confederate gunboats, which now hauled off and steamed up the bay.

The *Tennessee*, meanwhile, passed down the column of Union ships. Her lack of maneuverability prevented efforts to ram, but, as she went, her guns were firing on the Union vessels. Farragut wrote later that the Confederate ships inflicted greater casualties than did the guns of Fort Morgan.

The smaller Union vessels, meanwhile, concentrated on the remaining Confederate gunboats. The *Gaines* was hit several times below the waterline, and her captain tried unsuccessfully to make Fort Morgan. She got to Mobile Point about four hundred yards from Fort Morgan, where she went down. The *Selma* fired into the *Hartford* until the *Metacomet*, a double-end side-wheeler and the fastest Federal gunboat, attacked her and drove her into shallow water above Fort Morgan, where she surrendered. When her captain, Lt. P. U. Murphy, hauled down her flag, he and six crewmen had been wounded and two officers and six crewmen were dead. Farragut was not pleased that the *Morgan*, relatively undamaged, managed to reach the fort and was able to take refuge under its guns. That night she escaped up the bay to Mobile, where she participated in the defense of that city until it fell to the Union in May 1865.

The *Tennessee*, meanwhile, swept on, unable to ram any of the remaining Federal ships but firing at them and inflicting damage and casualties. Finally, after exchanging fire with the last pair of Union ships, she turned and gained the protection of Fort Morgan. Then Buchanan considered his next move. The remaining Union ships had now all passed safely into the bay and beyond the range of Fort Morgan's guns. At about 8:30, Farragut had his ships anchor about four miles up the bay. He intended to carry out a quick assessment of damage and allow the crews breakfast.

At this time Master's Mate James T. Seaver, captain of a Union support vessel, the sidewheeler *Philippi* (ex-blockade runner *Elia*), decided to bring his little ship into the bay, apparently to share in the glory. He had earlier sought permission to accompany the battle line but had been refused. Now he disobeyed orders on the excuse that he could render assistance to any Union vessel that had been disabled. Seaver kept to the far side of the channel, about two thousand yards from Fort Morgan, but the *Philippi* soon went aground, whereupon she was set on fire and destroyed by guns in the fort. Her crew abandoned her in haste, leaving behind one dead, a seaman.

The *Tennessee* remained quiescent, the ram's large propeller turning just enough to keep her stationary in the tide as Buchanan pondered his next move. Inspection revealed some damage, but the ironclad certainly was still battleworthy. Although many of his officers and men thought they had satisfied Confederate honor and done enough, Buchanan had every intention of continuing the fight. He assumed that Farragut would soon attempt to block the *Tennessee's* escape over the bar and perhaps mount a night attack.

Rather than wait to be attacked himself and vowing to "have it out," at 8:50 A.M., Buchanan ordered the *Tennessee* back against the entire Union fleet about 2 miles distant in what his crew had to believe was virtually a suicide mission. The Confederate artillerymen at Fort Morgan cheered the ram on. Mounting but 6 guns, the *Tennessee* would face 157 Union guns. Buchanan's hope was to catch the Union crews off guard, inflict what damage he could, then return to Fort Morgan and ground the *Tennessee* as a stationary battery to assist in repelling attacks on the fort. In any case, Buchanan did not want to see a repeat of what had happened to the *Virginia* in the James River, when she had had to be scuttled without a fight.

The *Tennessee* made for the larger Federal wooden ships, Union lookouts spotting the Confederate charge as soon as it began. At about two miles' range the *Tennessee* fired a bolt at the Union ships, but it did not hit any of them. Captain Drayton assumed that the ram would make for the bar and attempt to attack the squadron's vessels remaining in the Gulf, but Farragut knew Buchanan's target and ordered Drayton to ready the crew and immediately get under way. Farragut had Kinney signal to the iron-prowed *Monongahela* and swifter *Lackawanna* to "run down the ram." Signals also were run up on the flagship ordering all vessels in the squadron to join the attack.

Without delaying to hoist in his anchor chain, Commander Strong of the *Monongahela* ordered her to slip her cable and get under way. A few minutes later, Capt. John B. Marchand of the *Lackawanna* had his ship headed for the ram as well. At 6 knots, however, it would take the *Tennessee* at least one-half hour to reach the Union ships.

Strong and Marchand positioned their ships to ram the *Tennessee* on opposite sides. Although Buchanan tried to evade the attackers, both Union warships smashed into her at high speed, the *Monongahela* first and the *Lackawanna* about five minutes later.

Both sides exchanged fire, the Union cannon balls bouncing harmlessly off the sloping sides of the ram. The heavily armored and well-constructed *Tennessee* received little damage, but in the exchange both Union ships were damaged and took casualties. Although rammed twice, the *Tennessee* continued on course; Buchanan's target was the *Hartford*, now fifteen hundred yards ahead. Farragut, again in the flagship's rigging, observed events.

The monitor *Manhattan* now took up position between the *Hartford* and the *Tennessee*, but the *Manhattan*'s slow speed prevented her from being able to ram her adversary. She managed to fire just two shots, neither of which inflicted damage. Leaving the monitor astern, the *Tennessee* closed to within one thousand yards. Farragut accepted the inevitable and ordered his flagship ahead, full steam. Finally, at 8:35 the two ships struck one another a glancing blow on their port sides, each scraping the other. The *Hartford* let loose a broadside at only eight feet, but the shot barely dented the *Tennessee*'s armor. The Confederate ship had only two guns in broadside; one misfired, but the other fired a shell that exploded in the *Hartford*'s berth deck, killing five crewmen and wounding eight others. By now the entire Union flotilla surrounded the Confederate flagship, but she was still giving more than she was taking.

The collision with the *Hartford* pushed the *Tennessee*'s bow away from her prey, and Johnston decided to circle to build up speed for another attempt to ram. The double-turreted ironclad *Chickasaw* followed her, pounding away at the *Tennessee*'s stern gunport shutter until the end of the battle. At 9:45 the *Manhattan* joined in, and the firing at last inflicted serious damage on the *Tennessee*.

A shot from the *Manhattan*'s 15-inch Dahlgren ripped through the *Tennessee*'s side, tearing away 5 inches of iron and the more than 2 feet of solid wood backing it, although this was the only Union shot during the battle to penetrate the *Tennessee*. Meanwhile, the *Chickasaw*'s twin 11-inch Dahlgrens continued to pound the Confederate ironclad from the stern. Her shots cut the *Tennessee*'s poorly protected tiller chains. This necessitated the use of tiller tackle, but then the tiller arm was shot away, making steering all but impossible. The *Tennessee*'s stack also was knocked down. At the same time, shots jammed her aft gunport shutter.

The *Hartford* now carried out a turn and made for the Confederate ram. This maneuver, however, put the Union flagship on a collision course with the *Lackawanna*, which also had circled in hopes of another run at the *Tennessee*. Neither ship was able to change course before they collided. The *Lackawanna* struck the *Hartford*'s port quarter, cracking open her hull. Fortunately for Farragut, this hole was above the waterline, and the flagship was able to continue the fight.

Surrender of the CSS *Tennessee*, Battle of Mobile Bay, August 5, 1864. Naval Historical Center. NH 1276

Aboard the *Tennessee*, two crewmen were dead and Buchanan was wounded, hit by a ricocheting bolt inside the casemate. The *Tennessee*'s steering was gone, and she was almost dead in the water. Her ammunition was nearly depleted, and her bow, stern, and one of her port gunport shutters were jammed shut. Given these conditions, Buchanan, who had been taken below to the cockpit, authorized Johnston to surrender. The engines were stopped, and Johnston ran up a white handkerchief in place of the Confederate battle flag. Commander William E. LeRoy, captain of the *Ossipee*, saw the white flag. His ship was bearing down on the *Tennessee* with the intent to ram. LeRoy ordered engines reversed, but he was unable to avoid striking the ram a hard, although glancing, blow. LeRoy then identified himself to Johnston, who was standing on the ram's shield.

At 10:00 a boat from the *Ossipee* came alongside, and its party accepted the *Tennessee*'s surrender, carrying Buchanan's sword back to Farragut as the Union admiral had demanded. The sea portion of the Battle of Mobile Bay was over. It had taken three hours. Farragut later described it as "the most desperate battle I ever fought."[6]

The *Richmond Examiner* summed up the battle effectively when it noted: "It was a most unequal contest in which our gallant little navy was engaged, and we lost the battle; but our ensign went down in a blaze of glory."[7] This further test of ironclad vessels, steam power, rifled guns, and mines had a decided impact on future naval tactics. The battle was an important victory for the Union, ending traffic in and out of Mobile Bay in defiance of the Union blockade. It virtually ended blockade running in the Gulf. It also provided an important psychological boost, and no doubt assisted Lincoln's reelection campaign. But the city of Mobile remained in Confederate hands.

Farragut now turned his attention to the forts. One of the monitors took up position to the rear of Fort Powell. That night the Confederates evacuated and blew it up, which left Forts Gaines and Morgan. Cut off from assistance, their defeat was inevitable. Gaines surrendered on August 8.

An old friend of Page at Fort Morgan, Farragut sent him a message under flag of truce demanding the unconditional surrender of the fort to avoid unnecessary loss of life. But Page, who was disappointed, even shocked, that Farragut's vessels had been able to get past Fort Morgan into the bay and was angered by the surrender of the other two forts without his permission, replied, "I am prepared to sacrifice life, and will only surrender when I have no means of defense."[8] It took two weeks of bombardment to bring that about when, on August 23, Page again communicated with Farragut: "The further sacrifice of life being unnecessary, my sick and wounded suffering and exposed, humanity demands that I ask for terms of capitulation."[9] (The *Tennessee* participated in the attack; she had been repaired and then commissioned in the U.S. Navy on the 19th.)

The capture of Mobile Bay cost the Union side 145 killed and 170 wounded. The Confederates lost 12 killed, 20 wounded, and the crews of the *Tennessee* and *Selma* captured. On December 22, Congress created the rank of vice admiral, which Lincoln immediately conferred on Farragut.

Farragut made no effort to capture the city of Mobile and left that to the army. Not until March 1865 did Union forces mount an effort against Mobile. On the 12th a small Union tug, the *Althea*, being used as a collier and supply vessel, struck a torpedo and went down with two men killed and several injured. The *Althea*, later raised and recommissioned, was the first of seven Union vessels lost to torpedoes in operations against Mobile in a five-week period, including the river monitor *Osage*, sunk on March 29.

Against Mobile, Major General Canby had charge of forty-five thousand troops and Rear Adm. Henry K. Thatcher commanded the naval effort. Again, army-navy cooperation was excellent. The main land attack would move up the coast while a simultaneous diversionary effort went by water to a point on the opposite side of the bay to prevent additional Confederate troops from reaching Mobile. Union naval units provided transport for the troops and carried out resupply. Beginning March 21, Union gunboats supported the landing of troops at Donnelly's Mills on the Fish River, Alabama. Initially, Thatcher provided six "tinclads," all the light-draft vessels available.

With gunboats bombarding Mobile's forts from the water, the land forces worked their way to the principal Confederate position at Spanish Fort. A steady Union bombardment forced the Confederates to evacuate on April 8. Batteries Tracy and Huger, up the Blakely River from Spanish Fort, fell on the 11th. On April 12, Maj. Gen. Dabney Maury's ninety-two hundred Confederate defenders abandoned their defenses and the city surrendered.

Meanwhile, there was major naval activity along the South Atlantic coast. By 1862, Confederate Secretary of the Navy Mallory had decided to give up on the larger and more expensive seagoing ironclads and concentrate on smaller, coast defense types. In so doing, he hoped to obtain reliable power plants for them abroad. In all, the Confederacy laid down some forty of these warships, half of which were completed.

Confederate naval constructor John Porter produced a standard design for these warships, which was then sent to builders throughout the Confederacy. Porter's plan called for a 150-foot, screw-propelled, casemated, flat-bottomed vessel. The casemate would be completely armored and the hull partially, and the ship would mount six guns. Despite this effort at standardization, the resulting ships, called armorclads, varied widely in size, machinery, battery, and armor. They ranged in length from 139' to 310'. Armor also varied, from 2 to 8 inches, but all was of laminated iron. Most of the power plants did not come from Europe as Mallory had hoped but were salvaged from other Confederate vessels. Propulsion also varied from screw to paddle wheel. Although there was never a shortage of ordnance for these ships, they mounted a variety of types.

The first Porter-designed harbor defense vessel commissioned was the 150' *Richmond*, armed with 4 x 7-inch Brooke rifles and 2 x 9-inch Dahlgren smoothbores. Among other 150' ironclads were the *Chicora*, *Huntsville*, *North Carolina*, *Palmetto State*, *Raleigh*, *Savannah*, and *Tuscaloosa*. Among larger vessels were the *Fredericksburg*, *Jackson* (*Muscogee*), and *Milledgeville* (175'); *Charleston* and *Virginia II* (180'); *Missouri* (183'); *Columbia*, *Tennessee*, and *Texas* (216'); and *Nashville* (310'). Porter also designed the smallest, the *Albemarle* and *Neuse* (139').

The ironclad ram *Albemarle*, constructed at Edward's Ferry on the Roanoke River, dominated the North Carolina Sounds. She was the first of a two-ship class constructed by Gilbert Elliot; the other was the *Neuse*. Laid down in April 1863, the *Albemarle* was launched in July and commissioned in April 1864. She was some 376 tons, 139' between perpendiculars (152' overall) x 34' x 9', was driven by two screws from two steam engines with 400 horsepower, and could make in excess of 4 knots. She had a crew complement of 150 men. Armed with only 2 x 6.4-inch rifled guns, she had 6-inch armor. Damaged at launch, she was taken to Halifax, North Carolina, for repairs and completion.

ASSAULT ON PLYMOUTH

The *Albemarle* was completed in time to participate in Confederate Brig. Gen. Robert F. Hoke's assault on the Union blockading base at Plymouth, North Carolina. On April 17, 1864, the Confederate troops launched their attack. Union gunboats moved in to support the troops ashore but were taken under fire by Confederate shore batteries. Fighting intensified the next day as the Confederates pressed their attack, and a Union steamer, the *Bombshell*, was sunk. By 9:00 that night, however, the Southern assault had been halted. The fire from the Union gunboats had been a key factor in enabling the troops to repel the attackers; conversely, the Southerners needed support from the *Albemarle* to succeed.

The CSS ram *Albemarle*. *ORN*, series 1, vol. 8 (Washington, DC: Government Printing Office, 1899), frontispiece.

The Confederate ironclad, commanded by Capt. James W. Cooke, started down the Roanoke River from Hamilton on the night of the 17th but soon suffered mechanical problems. These were repaired, and she anchored above Plymouth at 10:00 P.M. on the 18th. Cooke was unable to establish contact with Confederate troops ashore but, sending out a boat, determined the location of the Union gunboats and shore batteries. The boat party returned to the ironclad after midnight to report that they could pass over the Union river obstructions because the river was up. Taking advantage of the darkness, at 3:30 A.M. on the 19th, Cooke weighed anchor and headed for the Union gunboats. Anticipating an attack by the *Albemarle*, the Union commander, Lt. Commander Charles W. Flusser, ordered the double-enders *Miami* and

Southfield lashed together for mutual protection and to maximize firepower.

When the *Albemarle* appeared, Flusser headed the two gunboats toward her, firing as they approached. The *Albemarle*'s ram struck the *Southfield*, commanded by Lt. Charles A. French, and tore a great hole, penetrating all the way to her boiler. Reportedly, the *Albemarle* came to rest ten feet inside the gunboat. The *Albemarle* backed engines on striking the *Southfield* but could not immediately pull free and was unable to reply to the fire poured into her by the *Miami*. At length, she pulled free as the *Southfield* went down.

Union shot was ineffective against the sloping, plated sides of the Confederate ram. The *Miami* withdrew under heavy fire, along with the small steamer *Ceres* and tinclad *Whitehead*. Flusser was among the Union casualties, killed early in the engagement. The *Albemarle* now controlled the water approaches to Plymouth and could provide important support to the Confederate forces ashore. Indeed, the situation resembled the advantage enjoyed by Union forces in the western riverine battles. Plymouth then fell to the Confederates.

Union naval forces, meanwhile, assembled below Plymouth. Commanded by Capt. Melancton Smith, the Union squadron consisted of double-enders *Mattabesett* (flagship), *Sassacus*, *Wyalusing*, and *Miami*, along with ferryboat *Commodore Hull* and gunboats *Ceres*, *Whitehead*, and *Isaac N. Seymour*.

On the afternoon of May 5 the *Albemarle*, accompanied by gunboats *Bombshell* and *Cotton Plant*, engaged the Union squadron off the mouth of the Roanoke River. The *Bombshell*, however, surrendered early in the action to the *Sassacus*, and the *Cotton Plant* withdrew up the Roanoke. Undaunted, the *Albemarle* continued on alone. One of her shots slammed into the starboard boiler of the *Sassacus*, killing several sailors and forcing her out of action. Union side-wheelers *Mattabesett* and *Wyalusing* continued to engage the Confederate ram, and the battle persisted for three hours until darkness halted it. The *Albemarle* then withdrew up the Roanoke River as the small Union side-wheelers, *Commodore Hull* and *Ceres*, took up position at the river's mouth to prevent her reentry into Albemarle Sound.

The *Albemarle* was a considerable threat to Union coastal operations. She easily outgunned the smaller Union coastal craft. Her shallow draft enabled her to escape the larger Union ocean-going ships, and Union officers noted her ability to turn quickly and that her speed of 6 to 7 knots was fast for an ironclad. They also reported that, in the May 5 battle, 100-pounder rifled projectiles broke up on hitting her ironclad sides. For months she dominated the North Carolina Sounds. Her commander was far less sanguine over her capabilities, complaining that she drew too much water to operate effectively in the Sounds and that she was slow and not easily controlled. Nonetheless, for the next five months the Union officers sought a way to destroy the ironclad. In July, twenty-one-year-old Lieut. William B. Cushing developed two plans and presented them in person to Secretary of the Navy Welles in Washington. Welles authorized Cushing to proceed to New York to secure the required equipment.

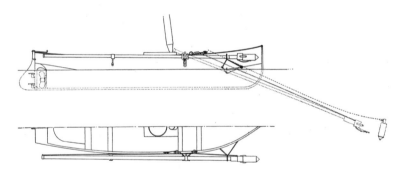

Cushing's torpedo launch—outline drawing. *ORN*, series 1, vol. 10 (Washington, DC: Government Printing Office, 1900), 623.

At New York, Cushing purchased two 30-foot steam launches and fitted each with a 12-pounder Dahlgren howitzer and a 14-foot spar and torpedo. The spar would be lowered by a windlass. Once the torpedo was in position under the target vessel's hull, a tug on a line released it, allowing it to float up under the hull of the ship. A second line activated the firing mechanism.

As the two launches proceeded south by the inland water route, one of them, *Steam Picket Boat No. 2*, developed mechanical problems and was forced to put ashore in Wicomico Bay, Virginia, where the Confederates captured her. The remaining launch, *Steam Picket Boat No. 1*, commanded by Cushing himself, arrived safely in the North Carolina Sounds on October 24. Cushing at this point revealed his intent to the crew and asked for volunteers; all seven men joined him.

Cushing set out on the night of October 26, but the launch grounded at the mouth of the Roanoke River. The crew finally freed her, but the mishap forced Cushing to postpone the attempt until the next night. The night of the 27th was dark and foul. Cushing was accompanied by fourteen men, the additional crewmen volunteers from the blockading squadron. *Steam Picket Boat No. 1* towed a cutter, the purpose of which was to storm aboard the picket vessel *Southfield* if necessary to prevent her from giving the alarm by signal rocket. The *Southfield*, sunk in action with the *Albemarle*, had been salvaged and then sunk in the river about a mile from the *Albemarle*'s berth.

A heavy tarpaulin helped muffle the noise of the launch's steam engine during her approach, and Cushing was able to get in close to the wharf before the alarm was raised. When discovered, he quickly ordered the cutter to cast off and make for the *Southfield*. At the same time, he ordered his own launch to get up steam and make for the *Albemarle*.

The Confederates now opened fire from both the ram and the shore. A large illuminating fire blazed up on the shore that enabled Cushing to see a protective boom of logs floating in the water around the ram. Coolly ordering his launch about, Cushing ran her full speed at the obstruction as he fired canister from his boat howitzer against the Confederates ashore.

Hitting it at high speed, the launch rode up over the log barrier and quickly was next to the *Albemarle*. Her torpedo boom with the charge at the end was then lowered under the Confederate ram. Almost simultaneously, a shot from the *Albemarle* crashed into the launch and the mine exploded. The resulting wash of water immediately swamped the launch. The torpedo had torn a gaping hole in the *Albemarle*, which now began to sink rapidly. She settled quickly and soon only her superstructure and smokestack were visible. Cushing ordered his own men to swim to safety. In the morning he managed to secure a skiff, and Cushing rowed her eight miles downriver to Albemarle Sound, where he was picked up by the USS *Valley City*. Only one other man aboard the launch escaped death or capture.

Attack by the U.S. Navy *Steam Picket Boat No. 1* against the CSS ironclad ram *Albemarle*, October 27, 1864. Naval Historical Center. NH 57267

The commander of the North Atlantic Blockading Squadron, Rear Adm. David Porter, heralded the event, and Union ships fired signal rockets in celebration. The destruction of the *Albemarle* was important indeed. It enabled Union forces to capture Plymouth and gain control of the entire Roanoke River area, and it also released Union ships stationed there for other blockade duties. Congress subsequently commended Cushing for his bravery and promoted him to lieutenant commander.

NOTES

1. Farragut to Jenkins, August 3, 1864, *ORN*, series 1, vol. 21 (Washington, DC: Government Printing Office, 1906), 403.
2. Alden to Farragut, August 5, 1864, ibid., 508.
3. Ibid.

4. Quoted in Loyal Farragut, *The Life of David Glasgow Farragut, Fleet Admiral of the U.S. Navy* (New York: D. Appleton and Co., 1879), 425.

5. James P. Duffy, *Lincoln's Admiral: The Civil War Campaigns of David Farragut* (New York: John Wiley, 1997), 247–48.

6. Charles L. Lewis, *David Glasgow Farragut: Our First Admiral*, 2 vols. (Annapolis, MD: Naval Institute Press, 1943), 2:280.

7. Quoted in Edward A. Pollard, *The Lost Cause: A New History of the War of the Confederates* (New York: E. B. Treat, 1866), 547.

8. Page to Farragut, August 9, 1864, *ORN*, series 1, vol. 21:563.

9. Page to Farragut, August 23, 1864, ibid., 537.

CHAPTER SEVEN

THE SEA WAR ENDS

THE LAST REMAINING major Confederate port for blockade runners, Wilmington, North Carolina, also was a principal overseas supply link for General Lee's Army of Northern Virginia. Both General Grant and the navy concurred with the need to close it. In early September, Secretary of the Navy Welles appointed Farragut to command the North Atlantic Blockading Squadron to replace Rear Adm. S. Phillips Lee, but Farragut declined for health reasons. Welles then selected the commander of the Mississippi Squadron, Rear Adm. David D. Porter, who was now available with the conclusion of the Red River Campaign.

The destruction of the *Albemarle* in October greatly facilitated Porter's plans to move against Wilmington. He was anxious to proceed, but it took time for General Grant to release the requisite troops. In December, Porter assembled the most powerful naval force in U.S. history to that point. Numbering more than fifty warships, five of them ironclads, it mounted more than six hundred guns. Along with the squadron were sixty-five hundred troops in two army divisions under Maj. Gen. Benjamin Butler.

The key to any assault on Wilmington was the destruction of the powerful Confederate defensive works of Fort Fisher, located on a narrow spit of land at the entrance to the Cape Fear River. If Fisher were in Union hands, blockade running would be halted. Fisher was a large work, fortified principally on the east facing the sea and on the south facing access to the river. The side facing the sea extended nearly three-quarters of a mile, while the southern face was about one-quarter mile in length. Porter and Butler worked out a plan according to which army troops would be landed on the beach north of the fort. Porter's ships would then bombard the fort, after which the troops would assault it from its north face supported by naval gunfire.

Confederate Col. William Lamb commanded some nineteen hundred troops at Fort Fisher. Well protected in a carefully laid out earthworks with shell-proof chambers, his men manned forty-four heavy guns in barbette mounts as well as numerous smaller pieces. The fort's land face to the north was protected by a high palisade of logs, beyond which the Confederates had planted land torpedoes.

The assault against Fort Fisher took place on December 24. Butler had suggested that the attackers try running a ship close to the fort and blowing her up under its walls. The former blockade runner *Louisiana* was selected and loaded with 150 tons of powder. While the Union transports waited some 20 miles away at Beaufort, well out of range of any possible side effects from the explosion, the ships of the fleet assembled about a dozen miles from the fort.

During the night of December 23, Commander A. C. Rhind and thirteen other Union volunteers undertook the hazardous assignment of positioning the *Louisiana* close to the fort. They managed to get her some 300 yards off Fort Fisher, set the powder trains to the explosive charges, and get away in the accompanying *Wilderness*. The *Louisiana* exploded as planned, shortly after midnight, but the blast did no appreciable damage to the fort. At daybreak the Union armada got under way. Porter's ships formed in line of battle in front of the Confederate works and about noon began a bombardment of some 115 shots per minute. Although most Confederate gunners in the fort were driven from their guns and sought refuge in the bombproofs, a few of the heavy guns did return fire. In fact, most of the casualties in the fort were caused by the bursting of several Confederate rifled guns. Among the ships in the fleet, the *Mackinaw* took a shot through her boiler and the *Osceola* was hit near her magazine and was only barely kept afloat.

Within approximately one and one-half hours of bombardment, however, the fort was largely silenced. Porter then maintained a continuing slow bombardment while awaiting arrival of the transports, which came up too late, however, to effect a landing that day. On Christmas Day, Porter resumed the bombardment at about 10:30 A.M. He continued this fire while Butler landed some two thousand of his troops away from the fort in boats be-

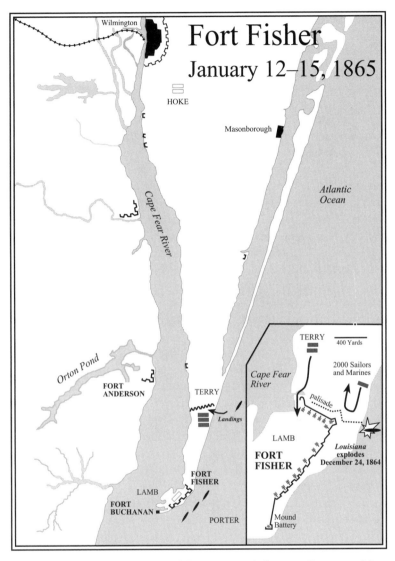

Fort Fisher
January 12–15, 1865

longing to the fleet, covered by some of the smaller warships. The landing was unopposed.

Meanwhile, Porter tried to find a channel through New Inlet to bring Fort Fisher under fire from the Cape Fear River. When the *Iosco* and some double-ender gunboats encountered a shallow bar, over which they could not pass, Porter called on Lt. Commander

William B. Cushing, who led an attempt in small boats to sound a channel. But under heavy fire and with one of his boats cut in two by a Confederate shell, even Cushing had to discontinue the effort. Late that afternoon some of Butler's men, protected by fire from gunboats offshore, got within several hundred yards of the fort. They reported that it was virtually undamaged by the naval bombardment. Following a brief demonstration but without attempting an assault, on December 27, Butler embarked his men and sailed back to Fortress Monroe.

Porter kept his ships in the Wilmington–Beaufort waters and periodically shelled Fort Fisher to stymie any Confederate rebuilding. Porter was furious at Butler and demanded that he be removed from command. General Grant agreed. Promising that there would be no repeat of the debacle, Grant wired Porter that the Union troops would soon return in greater strength and with a new commander. Maj. Gen. Alfred H. Terry was the new Union land commander. In communicating instructions to Terry, Grant praised Porter and stressed the need for close army-navy cooperation. In sharp contrast to Butler, Terry worked closely and well with his naval counterpart.

The second Union assault against Fort Fisher occurred on January 13, 1865. Porter had fifty-nine warships and Terry eight thousand men. That day Terry landed his four divisions, one of which was of U.S. Colored Troops, north of the fort and out of range of its guns. Terry then deployed his African-American force to build a strong defensive line across the upper neck of the peninsula to keep at bay some six thousand Confederate soldiers in the Wilmington area under Gen. Braxton Bragg and Maj. Gen. Robert F. Hoke.

On the 14th, as Terry's troops readied an assault from the northern land face, Porter's ships again bombarded its eastern side. This time Porter assigned each of the bombardment ships a specific target and ordered it to shell that objective until it was destroyed. He concentrated his most powerful ships to shell any Confederate guns so positioned as to impede the Union land attack. These ships included the *New Ironsides* and the monitors *Saugus*, *Canonicus*, *Monadnock*, and *Mahopac*. To increase the effectiveness of their fire, the Union ships anchored less than a thousand yards from the fort.

The bombardment lasted all day, and a few ships continued to lob shells into the fort into the night before departing. Reportedly, some three hundred Confederate casualties were inflicted. Certainly this barrage was much more effective than the previous shelling, disabling some of the heavy guns in the fort, opening breaches in the defenses, and severing wires used to detonate the land torpedoes. During the day the CSS *Chickamauga* fired on the Union troops ashore from its position in the Cape Fear River. But on the 15th, Cushing, in the USS *Monticello*, drove the *Chickamauga* back out of range.

On the evening of the 14th, Porter and Terry conferred aboard Porter's flagship *Malvern* and set the timing of the land assault on the fort for 3:00 P.M. on the 15th. Porter agreed to put ashore some four hundred marines and sixteen hundred sailors to assist the army by a simultaneous assault against the fort's sea face at the north.

The ships returned to Fort Fisher that morning and, shortly after 9:00 A.M., recommenced the bombardment. At about noon the naval landing detachments from thirty-five ships went ashore north of the fort. These men were hastily organized into four divisions, the marines under Capt. L. L. Dawson and the sailors under Commanders C. H. Cushman, James Parker, and Thomas O. Selfridge. Commander K. P. Breese had overall command. The men had never trained before and unfortunately were only lightly armed. The marines had rifles and bayonets, but the sailors had only pistols and cutlasses. Once they had organized, this force worked its way along the shore to where the north and east faces of the fort met. The Union attack, which was to have been simultaneous, did not work out; the soldiers, working through woods to their front, were delayed.

The sailors and marines, meanwhile, were moving up an open beach. Halting at the salient, and under heavy rifle fire from the fort, they attempted to charge through gaps in the palisade created by the naval gunfire. A great many of the attackers were cut down by canister and rifle fire, including two of their leaders, Lt. Samuel W. Preston and Lt. Benjamin H. Porter. Ens. Robley D. Evans, later to be a rear admiral, was wounded four times in the attack. Some sixty men broke through the palisade but that was as far as they got. Many of the sailors and marines then retreated in panic, some lying down and pretending to be dead until they could escape that night. In all, about a fifth of the attackers were casualties.

Presuming this to be the major Union effort, the Confederate defenders concentrated upon it. Exploiting the opportunity, three Union Army brigades on the land face pushed through the palisade and up the parapet. Many fell to Confederate artillery and rifle fire, but the survivors poured into the works. As they did so, the navy provided decisive gunfire support. Porter ordered the *New Ironsides* and monitors to fire on the traverses held by the Confederates, a number of these being cleared. The accurate supporting fire was of immense assistance to the troops ashore.

The fighting ashore was hand to hand and some of the bitterest of the war. The issue was in doubt until early evening, when Terry committed his reserve brigade. About 9:00 P.M. the Confederate garrison surrendered. The attackers had suffered some one thousand casualties, the defenders half that number. Among the Confederate casualties was Colonel Lamb, severely wounded. Three dozen Union sailors and marines were subsequently awarded the Medal of Honor for their role in the action.

Fort Fisher was the most heavily fortified position taken by amphibious assault during the war. Its capture was the last great Union maritime effort of the war and closed the remaining sea gate of the Confederacy. The fall of Fort Fisher was followed by a Union advance up the Cape Fear River and the capture of Wilmington, all of which starved Lee's army of essential supplies. Meanwhile, as Grant attempted to take Richmond and destroy Lee, Maj. Gen. William T. Sherman took Atlanta and drove east to the sea, cutting a wide swath through Georgia to Savannah. He then turned north through the Carolinas to join up with Grant.

In January 1865, Confederate Flag Officer John K. Mitchell, commanding the James River Squadron, launched an assault down the James River in an effort to take Grant's City Point supply base. Mitchell's hopes that a success there would turn the tide ashore were bolstered by the fact that Union warships had been withdrawn for the Fort Fisher–Wilmington area. Mitchell commanded eleven warships, including the three most powerful Confederate ironclads remaining: the *Richmond, Fredericksburg,* and *Virginia II.* The Union squadron in the river now only included one monitor, the double-turreted *Onondaga.* On January 23, as the powerful Confederate squadron approached, U.S. Navy Commodore William A. Parker withdrew his ironclad and ten small gunboats downriver.

The Confederate effort soon ended. That same day both the *Virginia II* and *Richmond* grounded trying to pass obstructions in the river at Trent's Reach where they came under fire from powerful Union shore batteries. Two other Confederate vessels, the gunboat *Drewry* and torpedo boat *Scorpion*, also grounded. The *Drewry* blew up when a Union mortar shell penetrated her magazine and exploded. The *Scorpion*, probably damaged by the same explosion, was abandoned.

The next morning, January 24, Parker returned with the *Onondaga* to Trent's Reach and opened fire on the Confederate ironclads with her 15-inch Dahlgren guns. Both Confederate ironclads sustained damage and withdrew upriver as soon as they were refloated. The last clash of the war between ironclads was a Union victory.

Not only did Grant's supply line remain in place, but he could continue his movement on Richmond. Recognizing the inevitable, and with his own position collapsing, on April 2, Lee abandoned Richmond and Petersburg and attempted to escape west. Cornered at Appomattox Court House, he surrendered on April 9, 1865. The Civil War was over. Some Confederate ground units held out weeks longer, and on the seas the Confederate raider *Shenandoah* continued to take and burn U.S. merchant ships.

It is difficult to overestimate the importance of the U.S. Navy in the Federal victory. Had there been anything like equality of naval force, there would have been no Federal blockade or at least it would have been ineffective, and Southern supply problems would have been greatly eased. There would have been no Federal outposts along the Southern Atlantic and Gulf coasts, and without these positions it is difficult to see how Federal squadrons could have operated. If New Orleans had remained under Confederate control, this fact alone would have had tremendous repercussions on the war, denying the North access to the sea for its goods and allowing the Confederacy to tap the resources of the Trans-Mississippi West.

Undoubtedly, Federal naval power shortened the war. Had it been prolonged, foreign powers might have entered the conflict or been inclined to provide additional military assistance to the South. The Civil War reveals that victory in warfare is a tandem of forces—in this case army and naval forces working together, supported by overwhelming industrial power.

Americans apparently had had enough of war, for the U.S. government soon disbanded the military. The army went from one million men at Appomattox to only twenty-five thousand by the end of 1866. The navy also languished. The second largest in the world at the end of the war in 1865, the U.S. Navy was, within fifteen years, inferior to that of Chile and every major European power.

Selected Bibliography

Anderson, Bern. *By Sea and by River: The Naval History of the Civil War*. New York: Alfred A. Knopf, 1962.

Bennett, Frank M. *The Monitor and the Navy under Steam*. Boston: Houghton Mifflin, 1900.

Bulloch, James Dunwody. *The Secret Service of the Confederate States in Europe*. 2 vols. New York: G. P. Putnam, 1884.

Canney, Donald L. *Lincoln's Navy: The Ships, Men and Organization, 1861–65*. Annapolis, MD: Naval Institute Press, 1997.

_____. *The Old Steam Navy: Frigates, Sloops, and Gunboats, 1815–1885*. Annapolis, MD: Naval Institute Press, 1990.

_____. *The Old Steam Navy: Ironclads, 1842–1885*. Annapolis, MD: Naval Institute Press, 1993.

Cook, Adrian. *The Alabama Claims: American Politics and Anglo-American Relations, 1865–1872*. Ithaca, NY: Cornell University Press, 1975.

Dalzell, George W. *The Flight from the Flag: The Continuing Effect of the Civil War upon the American Carrying Trade*. Chapel Hill: University of North Carolina Press, 1940.

Davis, William C. *Duel between the First Ironclads*. Garden City, NY: Doubleday and Co., 1975.

deKay, James Tertius. *Monitor*. New York: Walker and Co., 1997.

Duffy, James P. *Lincoln's Admiral: The Civil War Campaigns of David Farragut*. New York: John Wiley, 1997.

Elliott, Robert G. *Ironclad of the Roanoke: Gilbert Elliott's Albemarle*. Shippensburg, PA: White Mane Books, 1999.

Ferris, Norman B. *The Trent Affair: A Diplomatic Crisis*. Knoxville: University of Tennessee Press, 1977.

Hearn, Chester G. *Admiral David Dixon Porter: The Civil War Years*. Annapolis, MD: Naval Institute Press, 1996.

_____. *Gray Raiders of the Sea: How Eight Confederate Warships Destroyed the Union's High Seas Commerce*. Camden, ME: International Marine Publishing, 1992.

_____. *Mobile Bay and the Mobile Campaign: The Last Great Battle of the Civil War*. Jefferson, NC: McFarland, 1993.

Horn, Stanley F. *Gallant Rebel: The Fabulous Cruise of the C.S.S. Shenandoah*. New Brunswick, NJ: Rutgers University Press, 1947.

Jones, Virgil Carrington. *The Civil War at Sea*, vol. 1, *The Blockaders*. New York: Holt, Rinehart, Winston, 1960.

Kell, John McIntosh. *Recollections of a Naval Life*. Washington, DC: Neale Co., 1900.

Luraghi, Raimondo. *A History of the Confederate Navy*. Trans. Paolo D. Coletta. Annapolis, MD: Naval Institute Press, 1996.

Marvel, William. *The Alabama and the Kearsarge: The Sailor's Civil War*. Chapel Hill: University of North Carolina Press, 1996.

Merli, Frank J. *Great Britain and the Confederate Navy, 1861–1865*. Bloomington: Indiana University Press, 1970.

Morgan, Murray. *Dixie Raider: The Saga of the C.S.S. Shenandoah*. New York: Dutton, 1948.

Musicant, Ivan. *Divided Waters: The Naval History of the Civil War*. New York: HarperCollins, 1995.

Owsley, Frank L., Jr. *The C.S.S. Florida: Her Building and Operations*. Tuscaloosa: University of Alabama Press, 1965.

Porter, Admiral David D. *Naval History of the Civil War*. 1886. Reprint, Secaucus, NJ: Castle Books, 1984.

Ragan, Mark K. *Union and Confederate Submarine Warfare in the Civil War*. Mason City, IA: Savas Publishing, 1999.

Ringle, Dennis J. *Life in Mr. Lincoln's Navy*. Annapolis, MD: Naval Institute Press, 1998.

Roberts, Walter A. *Semmes of the Alabama*. Indianapolis: Bobbs-Merrill Company, 1938.

Roberts, William H. *New Ironsides in the Civil War*. Annapolis, MD: Naval Institute Press, 1999.

Robinson, Charles M., III. *Shark of the Confederacy: The Story of the CSS Alabama*. Annapolis, MD: Naval Institute Press, 1995.

Robinson, William M., Jr. *The Confederate Privateers*. 1928. Reprint, Columbia: University of South Carolina Press, 1980.

Scharf, J. Thomas. *History of the Confederate States Navy*. New York: Random House, 1996.

Schneeler, Robert J., Jr. *A Quest for Glory: A Biography of Rear Admiral John A. Dahlgren*. Annapolis, MD: Naval Institute Press, 1996.

Semmes, Raphael. *Memoirs of Service Afloat during the War between the States*. 1869. Reprint, Secaucus, NJ: Blue and Grey Press, 1987.

Shingleton, Royce. *High Seas Confederate: The Life and Times of John Newland Maffitt*. Columbia: University of South Carolina Press, 1994.

Silverstone, Paul H. *Warships of the Civil War Navies*. Annapolis, MD: Naval Institute Press, 1989.

Sinclair, Arthur. *Two Years on the Alabama*. Boston: Lee and Shepard, 1895.

Smith, Gene A. *Iron and Heavy Guns: Duel between the Monitor and Merrimac*. Abilene, TX: McWhiney Foundation Press, 1996.

Soley, James Russell. *The Blockade and the Cruisers*. New York: Charles Scribner's Sons, 1983.

Stern, Philip Van Doren. *The Confederate Navy: A Pictorial History*. Garden City, NY: Doubleday and Co., 1962.

Still, William N., Jr. *The Confederate Navy: The Ships, Men and Organization, 1861–65*. Annapolis, MD: Naval Institute Press, 1997.

———. *Confederate Shipbuilding*. Columbia: University of South Carolina Press, 1987.

———. *Iron Afloat: The Story of the Confederate Armorclads*. Columbia: University of South Carolina Press, 1985.

Summersell, Charles G. *The Cruise of C.S.S. Sumter*. Tuscaloosa, AL: Confederate Publishing Co., 1965.

———. *CSS Alabama: Builder, Captain, and Plans*. University: University of Alabama Press, 1985.

Symonds, Craig L. *Confederate Admiral: The Life and Wars of Franklin Buchanan*. Annapolis, MD: Naval Institute Press, 1999.

Taylor, John M. *Confederate Raider: Raphael Semmes of the Alabama*. Washington, DC: Brassey's, 1994.

Tucker, Spencer C. *Andrew Foote: Civil War Admiral on Western Waters*. Annapolis, MD: Naval Institute Press, 2000.

———. *Arming the Fleet: U.S. Navy Ordnance in the Muzzle-Loading Era*. Annapolis, MD: Naval Institute Press, 1989.

———. *Raphael Semmes and the Alabama*. Abilene, TX: McWhiney Foundation Press, 1996.

U.S. Navy Department, Naval History Division. *Civil War Naval Chronology, 1861–1865*. Washington, DC: Government Printing Office, 1971.

Wise, Stephen R. *Gate of Hell: Campaign for Charleston Harbor, 1863*. Columbia: University of South Carolina Press, 1994.

———. *Lifeline of the Confederacy: Blockade Running during the Civil War*. Columbia: University of South Carolina Press, 1988.

INDEX